Social Work and Integrated Care

Social Work and Integrated Care draws on the latest research, practice and theory to explore integration within both child and adult services. Although all the home nations in the UK view integrated care as a top priority within health and social care policy, many people continue to experience fragmented care. This book sets out the case for integration, considers the evidence of its impact, and discusses the implementation challenges that must be overcome.

Packed full of current examples of integration, from across the UK and internationally, and reflexive exercises which highlight practice issues for social workers, it provides the following key learning outcomes:

- An understanding of what is meant by integrated care and why it is seen as vital to a modern health and social system.
- A knowledge of the expected impacts in relation to improving the experience and outcomes for individuals and their families, addressing inequalities and promoting health and wellbeing and increasing financial efficiency.
- A recognition of the common barriers to integrated care and what such fragmentation can mean for individuals and their families.
- A critical review of key approaches to promote integration and their practical implementation.
- Reflection on the potential contribution of social workers and their own collaborative practice.

Providing a comprehensive and accessible overview of integrated care policies and practice, this book will help prepare social workers for the realities of collaborating with other professions and services. It should be considered essential reading for students undertaking their professional qualification and those who are in practice who are looking to improve their ability to collaborate.

Robin Miller is the Head of the Department of Social Work and Social Care at the University of Birmingham. His research interests focus on new models of integrated care between health and social care. He has previously worked as a social worker, manager and commissioner, and served on boards within housing and charitable sectors. He is the current Joint Editor-in-Chief of the *International Journal of Integrated Care* and an advisory group member of the European Primary Care Network.

Student Social Work

www.routledge.com/Student-Social-Work/book-series/SSW

This exciting new textbook series is ideal for all students studying to be qualified social workers, whether at undergraduate or master's level. Covering key elements of the social work curriculum, the books are accessible, interactive and thought-provoking.

New titles

Social Work and Social Policy, 2nd ed.
An introduction
Jonathan Dickens

Mental Health Social Work in Context 2nd ed.
Nick Gould

Social Work in a Changing Scotland
Edited by Viviene E. Cree and Mark Smith

Social Theory for Social Work
Ideas and Applications
Christopher Thorpe

Human Growth and Development
An Introduction for Social Workers
2nd Edition
John Sudbery and Andrew Whittaker

Counselling Skills for Social Workers
Hilda Loughran

Social Work and Integrated Care
Robin Miller

Social Work and Integrated Care

Robin Miller

Routledge
Taylor & Francis Group

LONDON AND NEW YORK

First published 2019
by Routledge
2 Park Square, Milton Park, Abingdon, Oxon OX14 4RN

and by Routledge
711 Third Avenue, New York, NY 10017

Routledge is an imprint of the Taylor & Francis Group, an informa business

British Library Cataloguing-in-Publication Data
A catalogue record for this book is available from the British Library

Library of Congress Cataloging-in-Publication Data
A catalog record has been requested for this book

ISBN: 978-1-138-48415-3 (hbk)
ISBN: 978-1-138-48416-0 (pbk)
ISBN: 978-1-351-05286-3 (ebk)

Typeset in Helvetica
by Swales & Willis, Exeter, Devon, UK

MIX
Paper from
responsible sources
FSC
www.fsc.org   FSC® C013056

Printed and bound in Great Britain by
TJ International Ltd, Padstow, Cornwall

Contents

Illustrations

Figures

Tables

Boxes

Acknowledgements

As ever, thanks to Vicki for her insights, encouragement and support.

Key terms

Integrated care: what people experience when services work together to ensure that they can plan their care to achieve the outcomes important to them.

Integration: the processes used to bring together professionals, services, organisations and systems in order to provide integrated care.

Professional: an individual who has training and experience to undertake designated roles within health and social care. This includes those who must register with a professional body and those who are highly skilled but may not require such registration.

Sector: the collective name for the bodies that fund, plan and deliver services in response to an identified public need. This includes social care, health, education, criminal justice and housing.

1 Why are we talking about integrated care?

Social workers know that a good quality of life requires the involvement of many people. This is primarily about the personal networks derived from family, friends, localities and communities of choice that provide emotional and practical support. Social work is about helping people to recognise and draw on the assets within such networks and to contribute in a relationship of reciprocity. For those who do not have strong informal networks, or face challenges of such scale that networks are not sufficient, then formal services can be necessary. These challenges may be related in part to a long-term disability, experiences of abuse or neglect, frailty or a mental health problem but will also have their roots in the multiple and enduring inequalities and discrimination with our societies. In the ideal welfare state, services to help with these challenges would be personalised and flexible so that the support is sufficient to what that person and their network requires to respond to the challenge. This would involve the services and the professionals who work within them being able to work constructively and seamlessly with the other services and professionals involved. All of us would want to provide and indeed receive support in which there are not gaps and uncertainties in what will be delivered and how it will be arranged.

Social workers also know that it is common for people not to receive person-centred and coordinated care. Most social workers will encounter on a daily basis examples of fragmentation between services: child and adolescent mental health services not responding to concerns from schools about the welfare of a pupil, hospital consultants not communicating with general practitioners about discharge arrangements for an older person, community psychiatric nurses not engaging with a housing support provider around a tenant's mental health. This leads to distress, frustration and anxiety for people and their families that add to the existing challenges. At its most serious, they can result in someone being left at risk of serious harm and abuse and their difficulties escalating to crisis point. As a social work professional this is also incredibly frustrating with precious time being lost which would be better spent positively engaging with a person and their family. The process of chasing, negotiating and in some cases advocating with other services is often stressful for the social worker concerned. Even more so then for the person whose needs are not being met and whose current and future wellbeing is affected. And sometimes it will be social work itself that can be the source of fragmentation.

The current focus in Northern Ireland, Scotland, Wales and England on integrated care is therefore something that should be welcomed by social workers. It reflects a global recognition of the harm that can be caused by services not being sufficiently coordinated and professionals not collaborating around the needs of individuals and families. In 2016 the World Health Organisation formally adopted a framework for integrated, person-centred health services. This highlighted that siloed health and care services 'undermines the ability of systems to provide universal, equitable, high-quality and financially sustainable care' and that it resulted in people being 'unable to make appropriate decisions about their own health and care, or exercise control over decisions about their health and that of their communities' (WHO 2016, p1). The framework statement later suggests that an integrated and people-centred approach to health and care services is 'crucial' if they are to respond to challenges such as 'global tendency towards unhealthy lifestyles, ageing populations, ... multi-morbidities ... rising costs' (p2). Similarly the European Commission stated that to break the 'vicious cycle of ill health and poverty' there must be 'multi-sectorial collaboration ... in order to shape the social determinant of health' (European Commission 2017, p21). This will include health and care working with organisations responsible for education and training, labour market, transport and food policies.

This realisation of the benefits of integrated care (and the damage of fragmented care) is however not new. Studies as early as 1969 by the University of Glasgow report that in relation to health and care of older people 'the development of each service was usually considered in isolation and that it could not be said that that there was an overall plan for the development of services' (Sumner & Smith 1969, p348). It suggests that a 'significant bar to co-operation was the division of responsibility without a clear-cut division of function. Too often this led to failure to develop a service because each side could argue that the other should do it' (p310). It is worth noting that at this time local authorities were responsible for community health services, so these disputes were often with the same organisation. Later in the book we will reflect on why it is has been so hard to translate this aspiration into reality (Chapter 3). In this chapter we will consider in more detail as to why integrated care is seen as a priority for all the home nations of the UK (and indeed in other parts of the world). We will conclude by reflecting on why this focus on better integration is of particular interest to social workers.

Think of a time when you required information and/or support from more than one organisation or service to achieve your objectives and/or cope with a difficult situation. This may relate to a health, social or educational issue, or something completely different such as planning a wedding, organising a house move or arranging to travel independently. What was important to you regarding the interaction with the various agencies and other people involved?

People tell us that integration is important

A continuing debate within public services, including social work, is how we define their overall purpose. This can seem a somewhat abstract discussion as surely the point of public services is to address the challenges that people face. However, we know from research that setting a clear expectation on what should be achieved is a vital starting point to prioritising how resources should be used and assessing the impact of any service. An important development in recent years has been the emphasis on the purpose being based on the outcomes that are achieved. This contrasts with previous decades in which the focus was on the amount and type of the service that was delivered. It used to be common that specifications would provide targets for the number of people to be supported, the types of interventions that would be available and the staff that would be employed rather than what difference the services had actually made to the people concerned. An example of this new way of thinking can be seen in the statement in 2006 by the Scottish Executive that 'Our national priorities must be about outcomes – the real improvements that people see in their communities and in their lives – better health, reduced crime and anti-social behaviour, an improved environment and increased educational attainment'. Similarly the Welsh Government (2017a) has defined its long-term aims in relation to what difference this will make to people and communities – 'prosperous and secure, healthy and active, ambitious and learning, and united and connected'. These are supported by a national framework which outlines the outcomes that would be expected to be achieved for people who need care and support, and carers who need support (Welsh Government 2016). Outcomes thinking has now permeated from policy to the planning and delivery of services, including how they are monitored and evaluated (see Box 1.1).

Another positive development is a recognition that people and families should be able to define the outcomes that are important to them. This again is a shift in thinking as previously it was professionals, managers and politicians who were seen as best able to decide 'what success would look like'. For example, in health care services there was more weight given to 'clinical outcomes', i.e. the outcomes that health care professionals have defined as being the expected benefits of an intervention or

---

Box 1.1 Inputs, outcomes and impact (Miller 2011)

Term	*Definition*
Inputs	All the resources a group needs to carry out its activities
Activities	The actions, tasks and work a project or organisation carries out to create its outputs and outcomes, and achieve its aims
Outputs	Products, services or facilities that result from an organisation's or project's activities
Outcomes	The changes, benefits, learning or other effects that result from what the project or organisation makes, offers or provides
Impact	Broader or longer-term effects of a project's or organisation's outputs, outcomes and activities

---

treatment. This meant that someone may have their health issue dealt with to the satisfaction of the doctor or nurse but still be left with a poor quality of life. Such health care measures are relevant as the professional will be able to identify aspects of a condition that are not understood by a lay-person but they are increasingly accompanied by measures of what matters to the individual concerned.

Social work and social care have been at the forefront of outcome-based approaches with many policy developments emerging from this sector. This includes 'co-producing' responses to challenges so that the objectives and offer relate to what people see as important and 'personalising' services so that the person is at the centre of care planning and delivery. These have led to governments investing more energy into understanding what people actually want from public services and their experience of receiving such support. Research has highlighted that such outcomes can be themed into three distinct areas (Glendinning et al. 2006):

Quality of life outcomes (or maintenance outcomes) are the aspects of a person's whole life that they are working to achieve or maintain.

Process outcomes relate to the experience that individuals have seeking, obtaining and using services and supports.

Change outcomes relate to the improvements in physical, mental or emotional functioning that individuals are seeking from any particular service, intervention or support.

Integrated care is a core element of achieving what people want from services (Box 1.2). Services being 'joined up' or coordinated is commonly highlighted when people are asked about process outcomes (Ellins et al. 2012). For example, have the professionals communicated about their individual assessments, are there multiple care plans with no overarching plan, and do the different interventions and support complement, duplicate or even conflict with each other? Beyond experience, many people will not be able to achieve what they want in relation to 'quality of life' or 'change' outcome without successful integration of services

---

Box 1.2 What people value from services

A comprehensive review of integrated working found that the aspects which are most valued by people accessing health and social care services include – responsiveness to their needs, relationships and partnerships with named key workers, communication between agencies, accessible information about complex systems, and care planning. It concludes that people and carers are less interested in the configuration of services but more how their own needs are addressed (Cameron et al. 2014).

A review of the evidence of 'what works' in supporting young care leavers' successful transition to independent living summarises that many such young people believe that services are not relevant to their situation, are bureaucratic and complex and will not treat them with respect or respond to their needs. It emphasises that to successfully leave care, planning should begin early, involve young people and those who support them and be collaborative. Continuity of workers helps to provide stability and security with achievements in one area of life giving confidence that there can be success in other areas too (Fauth et al. 2012).

around them. For example, for someone with a severe mental illness to be able to leave hospital after a time of crisis may require them securing somewhere to live, restarting benefits or employment, contacting previous networks, and engaging with new professionals and services. All of this requires coordination and communication to ensure that the necessary support is available at the right time.

The charity National Voices engages with people who access services, family carers, professionals and others to understand what is important from the perspective of people and their families. Their work has led them to conclude that people 'expect professionals to work together as a team ... and they want services to work together likewise ... to meet people's needs in the round' (National Voices 2012, p1). They have found that those who rely on multiple services in particular consistently say that they are looking for the system to both know them as a person and have knowledge of all the relevant supports and interventions to respond to their social circumstances and other conditions. Working with Think Local Act Personal (a national partnership in England of more than 50 organisations committed to personalisation and community-based support) they have developed a narrative of person-centred and coordinated care. This is now being accepted internationally as the standard by which we should assess the quality of integration (National Voices 2013): 'I can plan my care with people who work together to understand me and my carer(s), allow me control, and bring together services to achieve the out-comes important to me'.

The narrative expands on this overall standard through a set of 'I' statements which outline what someone would say if they experience integrated care in different aspects of their support. This includes out-comes, decision making, communication and care planning.

A lack of integration results in poor care

I was frustrated and upset when I read this report, though unfortunately I was not surprised. It is not about incompetent doctors, uncaring nurses or remote social workers; on the contrary the vast majority of them are highly competent, care deeply and desperately want to help. No, this report describes a health and social care system that is not working, that is let-ting down many desperately ill youngsters at a critical time in their lives. We have put the interests of a system that is no longer fit for purpose above the interests of the people it is supposed to serve. The system is fragmented, confusing, sometimes frightening and desperately difficult to navigate. Too often instead of helping young people and their parents it adds to their despair. It need not be like this.

Professor Steve Field (CQC 2014, p2)

The quote above comes from a report by the Care Quality Com-mission (2014) in England. It was outlining the experiences of young people with health conditions and their families regarding their transition from children's to adult services. It has been known for years that the transition process that is connected with someone becoming 18 and therefore defined as an adult is a diffi-cult time. Young people have to move on from a familiar set of services and routines which have been central to their quality of life. In many cases this will involve an end to relationships with professionals who they have known for many years and who understand their needs and circumstances. What they move on to will commonly be organised differently, with previous support options no longer available or accessible to them. Beyond university or college, there is no equivalent of school, and health care support will be provided by a range of specialists rather than through a paediatric service. The basis for assessment and eligibility for adult social care services is very different to that of children's, and dependent on which part of the UK they live there may be financial assessment for services.

The Care Quality Commission reported numerous failings in the way that transitions were planned and coordinated (see Box 1.3). This is despite numerous policy statements and good practice guidelines published over past decades. Many of the failings are not directly related to the individual quality and availability of adult services. These may of course be a contributory factor and a lack of resources can result in practitioners not having sufficient time to do their work thoroughly. The main difficulties were due to a failure to ensure that the process of transition was sufficiently integrated across and between adult and children's services. Key areas include – lack of clear information on what to expect, lack of clarity regarding professional roles, no identified coordinator to oversee the process and no transfer of previous assessments to inform the response of adult services. The impacts on parents and young people of such a poor experience are considerable. Parents told the CQC that they felt 'abandoned' by health and social care services at this most difficult time (p10). The Children and Young People's Health Outcomes Forum stated that such

> poor transition can lead to frankly disastrous health outcomes for both physical and mental health ... at its worst, poor transition leads to dropout from medical care for those with a long term condition, and deterioration in those with disabilities – both leading to unnecessary, costly and often distressing hospital admissions.
>
> (CQC 2014, p12)

A lack of integration is often found to have contributed to failings in care. In 2011 a *Panorama* documentary brought to the public

---

Box 1.3 Failings in the transition process (CQC 2014)

There was inconsistent and often poor information and preparation from children's services for young people and their parents about the changes they can expect as they move into adult services. This led to a lack of understanding of the process of transition. (p9)

Many of the professionals delivering care also told us that they were not clear about the process. Guidance and protocols for transition were often in place but not always being used, with some professionals unaware of their existence. (p9)

Some children's health or therapy services stopped at 16 but there was no adult service available until they were 18. This resulted in essential care being effectively withdrawn. (p9)

Of the young people and families that we spoke to, 50 per cent said there was no lead professional to support them through transition. Seventy per cent of the health and care staff we spoke to agreed. (p10)

Assessments to allocate funding for continuing health care were often completed by professionals with no previous connection with the young person and their family. This meant that key information was sometimes not available and decisions delayed. (p11)

---

attention the psychological and physical abuse of people with a learning disability at Winterbourne View. This was a private hospital which specialised in providing assessment and treatment services for people with a learning disability and behaviour that challenges. It could accommodate 24 people across two wards, the majority of whom were compulsorily detained under mental health legislation. People were funded by many different local areas in England and

Wales meaning that no one commissioner had a lead relationship. Many were placed far from home with about a fifth being referred by commissioners from over 120 miles away. There were multiple opportunities for services to respond to the abuse – for example over a 3-year period people attended Accident and Emergency on 78 occasions, the police were involved in 29 incidents involving people being cared for at Winterbourne View and 40 safeguarding alerts were made to the local council. Despite a whistle blower contacting the Care Quality Commission the regulator failed to sufficiently investigate their concerns. It is clear therefore that there was insufficient communication and coordination about these concerns between the various agencies and a more integrated approach could have resulted in the abuse being detected at an earlier stage. Even before they moved into this unit it is evident that people had suffered from fragmented care. The report by Mencap and the Challenging Behaviour Foundation provides a powerful account of the experiences of five of the people affected by the abuse – James, Chrissy, Joe, Emmanuel and Victoria (Mencap & Challenging Behaviour Foundation 2012). Insufficient collaboration between agencies resulted in their needs escalating to the point at which professionals no longer believed that they could be safely cared for within their current environment. This led services to then move them to new facilities which were far from their families resulting in further disruption and decline in their mental wellbeing.

Fragmentation between services is also a common finding of reviews within children's services. Vincent and Petch (2012) analysed 56 Significant Case Reviews (SCRs) and 43 Initial Case Reviews (ICRs) conducted in Scotland between 2007 and 2012. They note that a "significant amount of progress has been made in recent years to ensure that all agencies acknowledge they have a responsibility for child protection and this is evidenced in the numerous examples of good safeguarding practice .... identified in these SCRs" (p7). However, the Case Reviews consistently demonstrated that there was also 'confusion in relation to responsibilities in individual cases and there needs to be a shared understanding

---

Box 1.4 Fragmented care in safeguarding (Vincent & Petch 2012)

Too many drugs agencies were involved focusing on the separate needs of the parents rather than on how the drugs use of one may have impacted on the other ... Coordination of the role of different drugs workers was required in order to view the family's needs holistically. (p72)

Systems inhibited the free flow of information particularly between hospitals. This resulted in assessments and subsequent action being taken without those making the decisions being appraised of the full facts, for example the family's social history and the father's medical history. (p74)

due to systems within health at that time where a number of protocols and guidance existed for health professionals to follow. There were not clear pathways and protocols in place for appropriate and timely referral of possible physical abuse cases for specialist investigation. (p76)

---

of roles across agencies' (p7). This was connected with a lack of information sharing and poor coordination of assessments and intervention (Box 1.4). It is important to note that a lack of integration was not the only factor that led to inadequate responses to children and young people who were at risk. A lack of professional confidence in risk assessment, poor record keeping within agencies and inadequate alternatives for young people who could not stay in their family home also contributed.

Financial pressures are increasing

Across the UK and indeed the majority of the developed world, concerns are increasing about the ability of health and social care systems to cope with future demands for services. Partly this is due to demographic changes such as our ageing populations and a dramatic increase in the number of people who have more than one long-term condition. In Wales, for example, by 2039, there will be a further 44 per cent more people aged over 65 compared to 2014 and by 2035, the proportion of adults living with a limiting long-term condition is expected to increase by 22 per cent. The concerns are related to changes in our overall health and wellbeing. In England in 2018 it is estimated that 66 per cent of adults are overweight or obese which has significant impacts on their quality of life and costs the health and social care system around £5.5 billion per year. It is forecast the proportion of adults who are overweight or obese will increase further to 70 per cent by 2034 (LGA 2018). Northern Ireland is experiencing higher rates of mental illness with one in five people reporting mental ill health and a 19 per cent increase in people who died by suicide between 2014 and 2017 (Betts & Thompson 2017). There are similar pressures in relation to support for children and young people. In Scotland the number of looked after children increased by 36 per cent between 2000 and 2015. The number of children on the child protection register increased by 34 per cent between 2000 and 2015, with three in every 1,000 children under 16 now on the register (Accounts Commission 2016).

Social care services are experiencing particular financial strain. This is related in part to the demographic and social changes outlined above. These pressures have been amplified due to political decisions to reduce funding to local authorities and therefore social work and social care services. In Scotland in 2016–17, the revenue funding received by local authorities (i.e. the funding used for day-to-day costs), is 5 per cent lower than in 2015–16 (Accounts Commission 2016). This is a reduction of 11 per cent in real terms since 2010–11.[1] Despite this reduction, councils' total social work net spending increased in real terms from £3.2 billion to £3.3 billion between 2010–11 and 2014–15. Two-thirds of councils reported social work budget overspends totalling £40 million in 2014–15. Scottish councils identified homecare services for adults and older people as the service under most pressure. In England, government funding for local authorities fell by an estimated 49.1 per cent in real terms from 2010–11 to 2017–18. As a consequence, between 2010–11 and 2016–17 overall spending on social care reduced by 5.3 per cent (NAO 2018) despite the increase in need. English social care has a gap in 2018 of £1.44 billion between the estimated costs of delivering care and what councils actually pay. This is forecast to rise to £3.56 billion by 2025. The LGA (2018) estimated that local government will have a funding gap of £7.8 billion by 2025. Fifty-eight per cent of the demographic pressure relates to services for people of working age, including 39 per cent relating to services for people with a learning disability. In Wales there was an 8.2 per cent real terms reduction in funds available for day-to-day spending on health and social care between 2009–10 and 2015–16. This is forecast to result at a national level in a financial gap of £2.5bn by 2030–31 (Welsh Government 2017b). In relation to social care, the number of over 65s needing local authority funded domiciliary care or residential or nursing homes is predicted to rise by 47 per cent and 57 per cent respectively between 2013 and 2030. Other cost pressures included changes to legal duties and equal pay claims from social care workers.

The human cost of such financial pressures is enormous. Age UK estimated in 2018 that there were 1.4 million older people in the United Kingdom who do not receive the help they need. This included over 150,000 older people who need help with three or more essential daily activities and who received no assistance from either paid services or family and friends. Carers UK (2018) showed that 72 per cent of carers in England had suffered mental ill health (such as stress and depression) as a result of caring and 61 per cent had suffered physical ill health. It has been projected that relative child poverty will increase between 2012–13 and 2020–21 with families in Northern Ireland likely to be the worst affected due to lower employment forecasts and benefit changes (Browne et al. 2014). Areas which are the most deprived have been the worst hit by austerity with loss of income that is up to three times higher than the areas that have not been so affected (Beatty & Fothergill 2013). A review by the British Medical Association concluded that the impacts of

> substantial reductions in public spending ... has been to hamper progress in reducing inequality and poverty; poorer job prospects (particularly for younger people); a decrease in the number of households achieving a minimum income for healthy living; increases in relative child poverty; and increasing levels of material deprivation. These factors can impact negatively on health and wellbeing in the absence of strong social support systems. Vulnerable groups have been disproportionately affected, including individuals, families/children and older people on low incomes, as well as those unable to work because of disability or long-term illness.
>
> (BMA 2016, p1)

Better integration is seen by all the governments in the UK as a solution to these financial pressures. This is founded on three main assumptions:

1   Crisis avoidance: when people experience a crisis in their health and/or social condition they may not always be accessing the most cost-efficient services to help them address this crisis as there is not joined up information on what is available and/or access processes are not coordinated.
2   Rehabilitation: following a crisis the range of support that is provided is not sufficiently focused on enabling people to regain their independence and/or develop strategies to avoid crisis in the future. Input from a range of professionals and services is often required to deliver rehabilitation and resilience for the future.
3   Prevention: avoiding people's health and/or social situations deteriorating to a crisis point in the first place reduces their distress and their need to access more costly services. As it is not always clear who may be at risk of a future crisis, preventative

interventions need to work with the general population and engage mainstream housing, education, employment and other services.

Much of the focus has been on avoiding and/or ensuring timely discharge from hospital services of older people. Hospitals are one of the most expensive settings to provide care due to the intensity of staffing levels, the highly qualified workforce and the costs of maintaining buildings and related infrastructures. Extended hospital stays can have negative impacts on people's physical and mental wellbeing which is distressing for them and may lead to further use of public resources due to a loss of independence. In England there has been a particular focus on the issue of 'delayed transfers of care', i.e. when an older person is physically ready for discharge from hospital but an appropriate package of support has not been arranged for them in the community (Box 1.5). This has been calculated to equate to 20–25 per cent of all admissions and up to 50 per cent of bed stays (NHS Improvement 2018). The National Audit Office estimated in 2016 that the cost to the NHS of delayed discharges of older people was in the region of £820 million.

Lack of integration is seen to contribute to delayed discharges due to people's needs not being assessed in a timely manner, inadequate multi-agency planning of appropriate services and people waiting for support due to packages of care not being well coordinated. Fragmented services also contribute to the increasing numbers of people who are presenting at Accident and Emergency departments in the first place. For example, older people living in care homes are often amongst the highest users of emergency services in hospital. This is despite their living environments providing 24-hour social care and in some cases nursing support. Insufficient support from primary care services such as general practice and secondary care services such as geriatrics is thought to be a major contributor to care home residents accessing emergency services. Scotland also has a focus on improving discharge and avoiding admission with a series of 'new care models' exploring innovative

---

Box 1.5 Delayed transfers of care in England (NAO 2016)

1.15 million: bed days lost to reported delayed transfers of care in acute hospitals during 2015 (up 31 per cent since 2013)

2.7 million: our estimate of hospital bed days occupied by older patients no longer in need of acute treatment

11.9 days: average length of inpatient stay for older patients in 2014–15 (based on emergency admissions only)

5 per cent: percentage of muscle strength that older people can lose per day of treatment in a hospital bed

54 per cent: hospitals in our survey who told us that discharge planning is not started soon enough to minimise delays for most older patients

---

approaches. These include new ways to engage older people in their care and to integrate clinical health care services with community resources.

Integration is also seen part of the solution in reducing demand for more intense and therefore costly services for children, young people and their families. For example, Wales recognised that a common factor in families reaching crisis point was parental substance misuse. This significantly contributes to children and young people being found alternative places to live on a short- or long-term basis, as well as of course to the damaging effects on their wellbeing. The Welsh government therefore made a statutory requirement that Integrated Family Support Services (IFFS) are available across Wales (GSR 2012). Northern Ireland also recognised that supporting families at an earlier stage could prevent difficulties developing that could result in significant harm and a need for safeguarding interventions. They recognised that much of this early support to families was provided by the voluntary and community sector but there was not always good coordination between these agencies and with statutory services. The government therefore developed the concept of Family Support Hubs (Health & Social Care Board 2016). These have been introduced across Northern Ireland to provide a single and local point of contact for families. The Hubs do not directly provide services but rather are a signposting and referral service which promotes and coordinates an interagency response to support vulnerable families. Each Hub has an appointed lead agency to take responsibility for its coordination and operation.

What is the contribution of social workers to integrated care?

It will be evident from the sections above that for people and their families to experience integrated care will require commitment from all the many professionals and services within the welfare state. People will be unique in their situations and challenges and there can therefore be no set formulas for what collaborations will be required. That said, people with particular health conditions or disabilities may draw on similar services connected with these issues. For example, we can expect that people with a severe and enduring mental health problem are likely to have contact with specialist mental health professions including psychology, psychiatry, nursing and occupational therapy. They may also access targeted employment and housing support providers. Social workers will be a component of many of these specialist groupings and have the same responsibility as other professionals to facilitate more integrated care. Social workers in more generic teams should be also be working holistically and flexibly. This will include considering other resources and connections which could be of benefit to an individual and their family.

Beyond this shared responsibility with other professionals it can be argued that social workers have a particular contribution to achieving more integrated care:

Social workers are system thinkers: Social workers are the perhaps the profession that best understands the complex myriad of influence which affect people and their families. Their role is to engage those who are excluded to uphold their rights and advocate for access to the same opportunities as others in society. The International Federation of Social Workers describes this mandate as being to 'promote social change and development, social cohesion, and the empowerment and liberation of people'(IFSW 2014). Fulfilling this mandate requires social workers to have a solid grasp of the human behaviour and development theories which will enable change to occur at the individual, organizational, social and culture levels. Social workers see issues from different perspectives, empathise with those with alternative motivations, and seek positive resolution between parties who are locked in conflict. All of these suggest that social workers should have be able to objectively consider the underlying causes which result in fragmented care and suggest constructive alternatives to improving people's experiences.

Social workers are driven by values: The British Association of Social Workers (2014) underlines that the profession grew out of humanitarian and democratic ideals. It states that social work 'values are based on respect for the equality, worth, and dignity of all people'. It is these values that provide social work with its distinctiveness rather than a particular body of knowledge or skills (although these are obviously important to demonstrating its values in practice). This differs from other professions which do have ethical standards but which evolved principally to undertake certain tasks. Social work values emphasise people's right to self-determination irrespective of their chosen values and life choices if these do not threaten that of others. Participation by those who access services in all aspects of decisions and actions affecting their lives must also be upheld. Both of these values will underpin the person-centred nature of integrated care. Social work values also direct them to be concerned with all aspects of a person's life and work in solidarity with others to challenge social conditions. Again these are facilitators of integrated care.

Box 1.6 Integration within social work professional standards

Subject Benchmark Statement for Social Work (QAA 2016)

Contemporary Social Work increasingly takes place in an inter-agency context, and social workers work collaboratively with others towards interdisciplinary and cross-professional objectives. Qualifying degrees are required to help equip students with accurate knowledge about the respective responsibilities of social welfare agencies, including those in the public, voluntary, independent and private sectors, and to acquire skills in effective collaborative practice. (p7)

Knowledge and Skills Statement for the Assessed and Supported Year in Employment (ASYE) (Skills for Care 2015)

Social workers should work effectively and confidently with fellow professionals in inter-agency, multi-disciplinary and interprofessional groups and demonstrate effective partnership working particularly in the context of health and social care integration and at the interface between health, children and adult social care and the third sector. (p5)

Knowledge and skills for child and family social workers (Department for Education 2014)

Apply a comprehensive working knowledge of the role of other professions in the identification and prevention of adult social need and risk ... and effectively synthesise multi-disciplinary judgements as part of social work assessment. (p1–2)

Recognise own professional limitations and how and when to seek advice from a range of sources, including named supervisors, senior social workers and other clinical practitioners from a range of disciplines such as psychiatry, paediatrics and psychology. (p3)

> **The role of the Chief Social Worker (Scottish Government 2016)**
> has the competence and confidence required to provide effect-
> ive professional advice at all levels within the organisation and
> with the full range of partner organisations (p4) ... promote part-
> nership working across professions and all agencies to support
> the delivery of integrated services ... promote social work
> values across corporate agendas and partner agencies. (p7)

Social workers have a professional requirement: The ability to collaborate is a requirement throughout a social work career. It should be demonstrated from initial qualification, first year post-qualification, professional registration and senior practice leadership roles. Whilst the nature of this collaboration will vary dependent on social workers' career stage, there are many similarities in what will be required:

- Learning about the responsibilities, expertise and contribution of other agencies and professions. This enables the social worker to identify when another professional or service may be of value to an individual. It also means that the social worker knows when to seek their advice over relevant aspects of their own professional practice.
- Communicating successfully with those of a different professional background and contributing to the coordination of support. This includes undertaking the designated coordinator role and working positively as a team or network member.
- Articulating what social work can positively contribute and helping others to understand its legal responsibilities and professional abilities.
- Representing the social work perspective regarding a particular situation and constructively responding to challenge and disagreement.

These collaborative competences will require on-going reflection and development throughout a social worker's career. This is partly related to changing roles, for example if a social worker seeks promotion or takes on responsibilities for supporting students, or if they begin to work with a different cohort of individuals and families. Even in the same roles social workers will encounter new and uncertain contexts in which they may be unsure how best to enable integrated care. Reflection on joint working will be as important as that related to social work specific practices.

Have you heard integrated care (including through other terms such as joint working, collaboration, coordination) mentioned recently in the news? If so, were the issues that led to it being raised related to better use of resources, improving people's experience and/or avoiding people being subjected to harm (or was there another prompting issue)? Reflect (if relevant) on the manner in which social work is seen to contribute to either the problem or potential solutions.

Note

1. The 2016/17 figure does not include £250 million that the Scottish Government allocated to health and social care integration authorities to support social care, because the Scottish Government routed it through the NHS boards' budgets rather than council budgets.

Further resources

International Foundation for Integrated Care www.integrated carefoundation.org

The International Foundation for Integrated Care (IFIC) is a not-for-profit network that brings people together to advance the science, knowledge and adoption of integrated care policy and practice. It provides free webinars, international events and a host of other resources through its website.

Institute for Research and Innovation in Social Services www.iriss.org.uk

The Institute for Research and Innovation in Social Services (Iriss) is a charitable company working to enhance the capacity and capability of the social services workforce in Scotland by enabling access to, and promoting the use of, knowledge and research for service innovation and improvement. It has developed numerous accessible and evidence-based summaries of integrated care.

National Voices www.nationalvoices.org.uk

National Voices brings the voices of patients, service users and carers to bear on national health and social care policy in England. The organisation works with its membership to influence government ministers and departments, professional bodies and other organisations, to ensure that policy focuses on delivering what matters most to patients and service users, their families and carers.

Social Care Institute for Excellence www.scie.org.uk

The Social Care Institute for Excellence is a leading improvement support agency and an independent charity working with organisations that support adults, families and children across the UK. It has also worked nationally and locally in relation to integrated care.

References

Accounts Commission. (2016). Social work in Scotland. Available at: www.audit-scotland.gov.uk/report/social-work-in-scotland (downloaded 04.11.2018)

Age UK. (2018). *New analysis shows number of older people with unmet care needs soars to record high*. Available at: www.ageuk. org.uk/latest-press/articles/2018/july-2018/new-analysis-shows-number-of-older-people-with-unmet-care-needs-soars-to-record-high/ (downloaded 04.11.2018)

Beatty, C., & Fothergill, S. (2013). *Hitting the poorest places hardest. The local and regional impact of welfare reform*. Sheffield: Centre for Regional Economic and Social Research, Sheffield Hallam University.

Betts, J., & Thompson, J. (2017). *Mental Health in Northern Ireland*. Available at: www.niassembly.gov.uk/globalassets/documents/ raise/publications/2016-2021/2017/health/0817.pdf (downloaded 04.11.2018)

BMA. (2016). *Health in all policies: health, austerity and welfare reform*. Available at: www.bma.org.uk/-/media/files/pdfs/working %20for%20change/improving%20health/public%20and% 20population%20health/bos-health-in-all-policies-austerity-brief ing-2016.pdf?la=en (downloaded 04.11.2018)

British Association for Social Work. (2014). *The code of ethics for social work*. Available at: www.basw.co.uk/about-basw/code-ethics (downloaded 04.11.2018)

Browne, J., Hood, A., & Joyce, R. (2014). *Child and working-age poverty in Northern Ireland over the next decade: an update*. IFS briefing note BN154. London: Institute for Fiscal Studies.

Cameron, A., Lart, R., Bostock, L., & Coomber, C. (2014). Factors that promote and hinder joint and integrated working between health and social care services: a review of research literature. *Health & Social Care in the Community*, 22(3), 225–233.

Care Quality Commission. (2014). *From the pond to the sea: children's transition to adult services*. Available at: www.cqc.org.uk/ sites/default/files/CQC_Transition%20Report.pdf   (downloaded 04.11.2018)

Carers UK. (2018). *State of caring*. Available at: www.carersuk.org/ images/Downloads/SoC2018/State-of-Caring-report-2018.pdf (downloaded 04.11.2018)

Department for Education. (2014). *Knowledge and skills for child and family social workers*. Available at: https://assets.publishing.ser vice.gov.uk/government/uploads/system/uploads/attachment_ data/file/338718/140730_Knowledge_and_skills_statement_final_ version_AS_RH_Checked.pdf (downloaded 04.11.2018)

Ellins, J., Glasby, J., Tanner, D., McIver, S., Davidson, D., Little-child, R., Snelling, I., Miller, R., Hall, K., Spence, K., & the Care Transitions Project co-researchers. (2012). *Understanding and improving transitions of older people: a user and carer centred approach*. London: The Stationery Office, The National Institute for Health Research.

European Commission. (2017). *State of health in the EU companion report*. Available at: https://ec.europa.eu/health/sites/health/files/ state/docs/2017_companion_en.pdf (downloaded 04.11.2018)

Fauth, R., Hart, D., & Payne, L. (2012). *Supporting care leavers' successful transition to independent living*. Available at: www. ncb.org.uk/sites/default/files/uploads/documents/Research_re ports/ncb_rsch_9_final_for_web.pdf (downloaded 04.11.2018)

Glendinning, C., Clarke, S., Hare, P., Kotchetkova, I., Maddison, J., & Newbronner, L. (2006). *Outcomes-focused services for older people*. Available at: www.scie.org.uk/publications/knowledgere views/kr13.pdf (downloaded 04.11.2018).

Government Social Research. (2012). *Evaluation of the Integrated Family Support Service. First interim report*. Available at: https:// gov.wales/statistics-and-research/evaluation-integrated-family-support-service/?lang=en (downloaded 04.11.2018)

Health & Social Care Board. (2016). *Family Support Hubs in North-ern Ireland*. Available at: www.cypsp.hscni.net/wp-content/ uploads/2016/06/SCIE-Family-Support-Hub-Review-2016.pdf (downloaded 04.11.2018)

International Federation of Social Workers. (2014). *Global definition of social work*. Available at: www.ifsw.org/what-is-social-work/ global-definition-of-social-work/ (downloaded 04.11.2018)

Laming, H. (2003). *The Victoria Climbie inquiry*. Available at: www. gov.uk/government/publications/the-victoria-climbie-inquiry-report-of-an-inquiry-by-lord-laming (downloaded 04.11.2018)

LGA. (2018). *The lives we want to lead: the LGA green paper for adult social care and wellbeing*. Available at: www.local.gov.uk/lives-we-want-lead-lga-green-paper-adult-social-care (downloaded 04.11.2018)

Mencap & Challenging Behaviour Foundation. (2012). *Out of sight: stopping the neglect and abuse of people with a learning disability*. Available at: www.mencap.org.uk/sites/default/files/2016-08/Out-of-Sight-Report.pdf (downloaded 04.11.2018)

Miller, E. (2011). *Measuring personal outcomes: challenges and strategies*. Glasgow: Institute for Research and Innovation in Social Services.

National Audit Office. (2016). *Discharging older patients from hospital*. Available at: www.nao.org.uk/report/discharging-older-patients-from-hospital/

National Audit Office. (2018). *The health and social care interface*. Available at: www.nao.org.uk/report/the-health-and-social-care-interface/ (downloaded 04.11.2018)

National Voices. (2012). *Integrated care: what do patients, services users and carers want?* Available at: www.nationalvoices.org.uk/publications/our-publications/integrated-care-what-do-patients-service-users-and-carers-want (downloaded 04.11.2018)

National Voices. (2013). *Narrative for person centred and coordinated care*. Available at: www.nationalvoices.org.uk/publications/our-publications/narrative-person-centred-coordinated-care (downloaded 04.11.2018)

NHS Improvement. (2018). *Guide to reducing long term stays*. Available at: https://improvement.nhs.uk/resources/guide-reducing-long-hospital-stays/ (downloaded 04.11.2018)

QAA. (2016). *QAA subject benchmark statement for social work*. Available at: www.qaa.ac.uk/docs/qaa/subject-benchmark-statements/sbs-social-work-16.pdf?sfvrsn=1d95f781_6 (downloaded 04. 11.2018)

Scottish Executive. (2006). *Transforming public services: the next phase of reform*. Available at: www2.gov.scot/Publications/2006/06/15110925/0 (downloaded 04.11.2018)

Scottish Government. (2016). *The role of the Chief Social Worker*. Available at: www.gov.scot/publications/role-chief-social-work-officer/ (downloaded 04.11.2018)

Skills for Care. (2015). *Knowledge and skills statement for the assessed and supported year in employment*. Available at: www.skillsforcare.org.uk/Learning-development/social-work/asye-adults/The-Assessed-and-Supported-Year-in-Employment-Adults.aspx (downloaded 04.11.2018)

Sumner, G., & Smith, R. (1969). *Planning local authority services for the elderly*. London: George, Allen & Unwin. Cited in Wistow, G. (2012). Still a fine mess? Local government and the NHS 1962 to 2012. *Journal of Integrated Care*, 20(2), 101–114.

Vincent, S., & Petch, A. (2012). *Audit and analysis of Significant Case Reviews*. Available at: www.iriss.org.uk/resources/reports/audit-and-analysis-significant-case-reviews (downloaded 04.11.2018)

Welsh Government. (2016). *Measuring national well-being: a report on the national outcomes framework for people who need care and support, and carers who need support*. Available at: https://socialcare.wales/research-and-data/research-on-care-finder/the-national-outcomes-framework-for-people-who-need-care-and-support-and-carers-who-need-support (downloaded 04.11.2018)

Welsh Government. (2017a). *Prosperity for All: the national strategy*. Available at: https://gov.wales/docs/strategies/181002-prosperity-for-all-annual-report-en.pdf (downloaded 04.11.2018)

Welsh Government. (2017b). *Parliamentary review of health and social care in Wales. Interim report*. Available at: https://beta.gov.wales/sites/default/files/publications/2017-07/170714-review-interim-report-en.pdf (downloaded 04.11.2018)

World Health Organization. (2016). Framework on integrated, people-centred health services. Report by the Secretariat. Geneva: WHO. Available at: www.who.int/servicedeliverysafety/areas/people-centred-care/en/on (downloaded 04.11.2018)

2 National policies for integrated care

Chapter 1 outlined that better integration is a focus for all the national governments in the UK as a means to respond to the expectations of their citizens, improve the quality of services and to cope with rising demands and financial pressures. The main focus for frontline social workers is generally the network of services in their immediate locality, their core legal duties and their organisation's procedures. This is understandable as these will principally be the guide for their work which will enable them to provie positive support to individual and their families. The broader legal responsibilities of their organisations and strategic partnership arrangements can seem distant and therefore of less relevance. But as we also saw in Chapter 1, social workers have a professional duty to collaborate with other professions and services, and to represent the interests of the individuals and communities that they support. Understanding the wider policy environment in which social work operates is part of fulfilling these duties. It helps professionals to interpret the vision set out by their local partnerships and the organisational procedures that follow. It enables them to contribute to engagement opportunities around future strategies to respond to the needs of local populations. It can facilitate collaboration with colleagues within other sectors through recognising the shared context in which they work. In this chapter, we will therefore consider how each of the four home nations are approaching the aspiration of more integrated care within national policy. Our focus will be the main legislation, partnership infrastructure and integration policies. We will consider a sample of integrated care initiatives that relate to specific populations as examples of what accompanies the main polices.

It is worth first noting general similarities and differences between the systems within the UK. The type and range of services that are delivered are broadly comparable. All of them have for example: schools, colleges and universities as their main venues for learning; hospitals, general practices and community services as their main deliverers of heath care; and social care provided by a range of statutory and independent agencies. Statutory social work is generally the responsibility of local authorities other than in Northern Ireland where it falls to the Health and Social Care Trusts. The professionals who work within these services share similar roles and qualification requirements. Nurses, doctors and dentists have the same regulatory body across the UK unlike teachers and social workers which are country-specific. All of them have mixed economies of welfare which will include public, private, voluntary and informal provision. The balance within these sectors does vary however. England has been the keenest to introduce independent providers for services that have traditionally been within the public sector. This includes academy and free schools, tendering for NHS services and the spinning out of community health and social care services into social enterprises. The funding structures are broadly similar with the overall income received by home nations from the UK determined by the Barnett formula. Decisions to increase or decrease the funding for the NHS in England will lead to similar changes in the home nations but it is for their governments to decide how then to spend this funding or find the required savings. Charges to people accessing services vary in some instances – for example only in England do people have to pay for NHS prescriptions and in Scotland there is free personal care.

As a social worker you may wish to practice in different parts of the UK to develop your skills and career or in response to other changes in your personal circumstances. You may also support people who have lived previously in another home nation. Understanding the main differences between the home nations' approaches to key public services can therefore be helpful. Spend a moment writing down what you think is similar or different regarding how the home nations approach social care, health services and education.

Scotland

improve the quality and consistency of services for patients, carers, service users and their families; to provide seamless, joined up quality health and social care services in order to care for people in their homes or a homely setting where it is safe to do so; and to ensure resources are used effectively and efficiently to deliver services that meet the increasing number of people with longer term and often complex needs, many of whom are older.

(Scottish Parliament 2013, p1)

Increasing pressures on health and social care services and limited success with previous attempts to integrate health and social care led the Scottish Parliament to approve The Public Bodies (Joint Working) (Scotland) Bill on 28 May 2013. The aspirations of the Bill (see above) combines better outcomes for individuals and families with more effective and efficient use of resources. The Bill has introduced a set of integrated planning principles to guide future direction and implementation of health and social care services (Audit Scotland 2015). These rights-based principles include – to respect the right and dignity of 'service users'; to be planned and led locally in a way which is engaged with the community; to take account of the participation by service users in the community in which service users live; and protect and improve the safety of service users. NHS boards in Scotland are responsible for the planning and delivery of health care services (other than general practice which are owned by general practitioners). They and local authorities are required to develop a local 'integration scheme' which outlines how they will jointly achieve a national set of health and wellbeing outcomes (Scottish Government 2015) (Box 2.1).

Local integration schemes must include the development of an Integration Authority. Integration Authorities bring together the oversight, planning and funding of adult social care services, adult primary care and community health services and some hospital services. The hospital services under the remit of the local integration schemes include accident and emergency, geriatric medicine, palliative care and addiction and substance dependency services. Other hospital services continue to be overseen directly by NHS boards. Local areas can decide to include other activities under the direction of Integration Authorities such as criminal justice social work and children's health and social care services.

Box 2.1 National Health and Wellbeing Outcomes in Scotland (Scottish Government 2015)

- **Outcome 1:** People are able to look after and improve their own health and wellbeing and live in good health for longer
- **Outcome 2:** People, including those with disabilities or long-term conditions, or who are frail, are able to live, as far as reasonably practicable, independently and at home or in a homely setting in their community
- **Outcome 3.** People who use health and social care services have positive experiences of those services, and have their dignity respected
- **Outcome 4.** Health and social care services are centred on helping to maintain or improve the quality of life of people who use those services
- **Outcome 5.** Health and social care services contribute to reducing health inequalities
- **Outcome 6.** People who provide unpaid care are supported to look after their own health and wellbeing,

---

> including to reduce any negative impact of their caring role on their own health and wellbeing
> - **Outcome 7.** People using health and social care services are safe from harm
> - **Outcome 8.** People who work in health and social care services feel engaged with the work they do and are supported to continuously improve the information, support, care and treatment they provide
> - **Outcome 9.** Resources are used effectively and efficiently in the provision of health and social care services

Integration authorities can follow one of two models: an Integration Joint Board (also called a body corporate) or a 'Lead Agency'. Joint Boards and Lead Agencies are responsible for developing a strategic commissioning plan. This outlines how the integrated budgets will be used to achieve the health and wellbeing outcomes. The plan must be reviewed every three years and detail the funding and services overseen by the Integration Authority.

Integration Joint Board: The local authority and NHS Board delegate responsibilities and the connected budgets for the planning and resourcing of mandated and additional health and social care services. Integration Joint Boards are comprised of voting and non-voting members. There are at least six voting members who are local authority councillors and NHS board members (ideally non-executive directors). The Board is allowed to appoint more members if it so chooses but these must be split evenly between nominees from the local authorities and the NHS. Non-voting members attend meetings but do not have a final say on the decisions made by the Board. Non-voting members should include people with lived experience, at least one representative of the voluntary and community sector, a general practice representative, and the Chief Social Worker from the local authority. Of the 31 Integration Authorities, 30 have selected to follow the Joint Board model.

Lead Agency: Either the local authority or the NHS Board takes lead responsibility for the planning and delivery of integrated health and social care services. Staff and funding connected with the direct services and planning functions are transferred to the lead agency from the other partner. The Chief Executive of the lead agency is responsible for organising the strategic group and developing an overall vision and implementation plan. NHS Highland and Highland Council are the only area to have used the lead agency model. Under the Highland Partnership, NHS Highland is the lead agency for adult health and care services and Highland Council is the lead agency for children's community health and social care services.

Integration Authorities are further required to develop more localised planning arrangements to influence their overall strategy. There is flexibility in how these are configured, but they must bring together identified stakeholder groups including those with lived experience (including carers), housing, health and social care professionals and representatives of the voluntary and community sector. Each Integration Authority must establish at least two localities but beyond that requirement is considerable flexibility. For example in 2015 the Edinburgh Integration Joint Board had four localities (with an average population of 120,000) whereas the Shetland Integration Joint Board had seven localities (with an average population of 4,000) (Burgess 2016). A review of the processes for consulting with their 'localities' must be included in the Integration Authorities' annual performance reports along with the proportion of the total budget spent in each locality specified.

Before the Public Bodies (Joint Working) Act 2014 there had already been considerable interest in the potential of intermediary care. In Scotland this is used as an 'umbrella' term. It describes approaches seeking to provide a set of 'bridges' at key points of transition in a person's life. These include those transitioning from hospital to home (and from home to hospital) and from illness or injury to recovery and independence (Joint Improvement Team 2012, p5). Common services include – 'virtual wards' where people receive intense health care support at home; rapid response rehabilitation teams; short-term care in community hospitals or care homes; and reablement services delivered through home care. The Scottish government sees intermediary care as making three main contributions (Scottish Government 2018):

1. Help people avoid going into hospital unnecessarily
2. Help people to be as independent as possible after a stay in hospital
3. Prevent people from having to move into a care home until they really need to

Five demonstrator sites were set up in 2009/10 to develop learning and practical tools for implementation of intermediary care. A national framework was launched in 2012 to provide a consistency in vision about the potential and purpose of intermediary care. This sets out the building blocks required for a good quality of intermediary care. It includes – anticipatory care planning to help people make informed decisions and plan through future changes in their care; holistic assessments that build on the principles of personalisation; coordination at strategic and operational (i.e. at the level of the person) levels; and multi-agency and multi-professional working.

In relation to services for children and young people there are two elements of the Children and Young People (Scotland) Act 2014 which relate specifically to integration (Kidner 2013). The first is the requirement for local authorities and health boards to develop joint children's services plans every three years. These must include services which are specifically targeted for children and other services which are 'capable' of having a significant effect on children and young people's wellbeing. Local areas have to report each year on progress with their joint plan to Scottish Ministers. The Act has also put in statute a requirement for coordinated support of children and young people, including every child having a named person. This person will act as a single point of contact for any concerns regarding the individual and be a source of advice and guidance to families. The Act also requires the development of single plans for children and young people with wellbeing needs, and the guidance outlines expectation on lead professionals for children and young people with complex needs.

Audit Scotland reviewed the new integrated care arrangement in 2015. They found widespread support for the principles of more integrated care and the general direction of travel within the legislation and associated policies. However, they reported difficulties in some areas in the development of their strategic plans (these were due in April 2016). These were principally related to disagreements about local funding arrangements and national uncertainty about some funding streams. These, along with wider issues relating to a lack of workforce skills and capacity in key professions and services, meant that Audit Scotland were not yet confident that the expected transformation in health and care by Integration Authorities would be achieved.

During the development of the Public Bodies (Joint Working) (Scotland) Act there were concerns regarding the potential of children's services getting lost in the new arrangements. This was on the basis that much of the focus appeared to be improving outcomes for adults, and in particular older adults. Brock and Everingham (2018) were commissioned to research integration within children's services. They report that the general view was that the new structures were not unhelpful and that they found examples of them supporting local commitment to more integrated working in children's services even if they will not necessarily be the solution for areas in which there is not such a history and culture of collaboration. Furthermore, there was a strong consensus that even if there were concerns regarding structures there was no appetite for further change and that priority was a period of stability. The main facilitator for integrated care within children's services was not the planning requirements but Getting it Right for Every Child – they report that it is 'viewed as providing a unifying practice framework, shared language and approach to working together to manage risk and address prevention and early intervention, across a multidisciplinary team and operational and strategic contexts' (p6). Brock and Everingham (2018) also highlight the importance of the Chief Social Work Officer to ensuring there is a strong social work contribution to the integrated planning discussions. This, and their concerns regarding the capacity of Chief Social Work Officers to undertake this alongside their other duties, is emphasised by Audit Scotland (2016).

Wales

> Individuals, their families and carers may require care and/or support from more than one professional or organisation. Where this is the case, the care and support they receive should be effectively coordinated and delivered to meet their specific needs. The purpose of Part 9 of the Social Services and Well-being (Wales) Act 2014 is to ensure there are co-operation and partnership arrangements in place to enable this.
>
> (Welsh Government 2015a, p14)

Whilst the purpose of the Social Services and Well-being (Wales) Act 2014 was predominantly on setting out the future delivery of social care, Part 9 had a particular focus on integration across health and social care. Local Authorities are required to promote co-operation with their relevant partners in order to promote the wellbeing of children, adults who require care and support, and family carers. In turn, other partners have a duty to supply information and co-operate with local authorities in relation to their social care functions. New bodies, called Regional Partnership Boards, were established to oversee strategic planning and partnership between health and social care.

Each Regional Partnership Board has one Health Board and between one and six Local Authorities in line with nationally directed partnership arrangements. For example, Gwent Regional Board – included Aneurin Bevan University Health Board and Monmouthshire, Newport, Caerphilly, Torfaen and Blaenau Gwent local authorities. Health Boards are responsible for the delivery of hospital, mental health and community health services and planning across the local health system. The Regional Partnership Boards must also have a lay member, a representative of the voluntary and community sector, and a representative of care providers. Boards must ensure that people who use services and their families are actively engaged in their work. This should include gaining the views of Citizen Panels. These panels were set up for adults, and for young people, in the North, South East and South West of Wales to help the government understand what had changed following the introduction of the 2014 Act.

Regional Partnership Boards must prioritise integration for the following populations or services – older people with complex needs and long-term conditions; families in crisis due to substance misuse; people with a learning disability; children with complex needs due to disability or illness; and family carers (see Figure 2.1). Other priority populations can be developed in line with the joint population assessment completed within each region. Boards are required to pool funding in relation to the

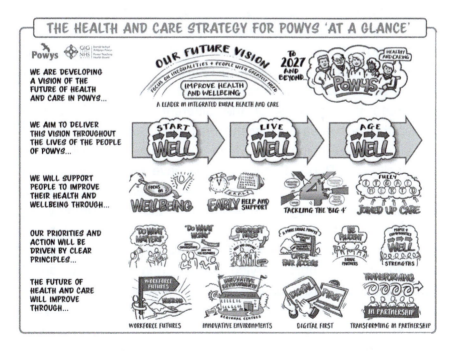

Figure 2.1 Regional Partnership Board priorities in Powys (Powys Regional Partnership Board 2018)

commissioning of services from residential and nursing homes and grants they have been provided for Integrated Family Support Services. Regions can also decide to pool other funds and/or delegate functions across health and social care in line with Section 33 of the National Health Service (Wales) Act 2006. The Welsh government launched the Intermediate Care Fund (to become the Integrated Care Fund in 2018/19) (Welsh Government 2018a). This allocates capital and revenue funding to the Regional Partnership Boards to support collaboration across health, social care, housing and the voluntary sector (Welsh Government 2018b) in relation to older people, children and adults with disabilities and people with autism. In 2018/19, a proportion of its £50 million revenue funding was used to support the national rollout of a common IT system across health and social care.

The Well-being of Future Generations (Wales) Act 2015 has a broader vision than health and social care. Its aim is to improve and sustain the social, economic, environmental and cultural well-being of Wales. The Act gives corresponding duties to a range of public institutions which include local authorities and health boards and national bodies responsible for parks, sport and culture. It sets out seven Wellbeing Goals (see Box 2.2). A Public Service Board has been created in each Local Authority area to coordinate the activities of the different bodies. These must assess the local area against the Wellbeing Goals and then publish a Local Well-being Plan which shows how they will improve local wellbeing. Public Service Boards have four statutory members – the local authority, the local health board, fire and rescue authorities for the geographic areas within the local authority, and the Natural Resources Body for Wales. Police, probation and a voluntary sector representative must also be invited but do not need to accept. Public Service Boards then publish an annual report setting out progress against their Wellbeing Plan.

Integrated Family Support Services were established by the Children and Families (Wales) Measure 2010. This reflected the commitment of the Welsh Assembly Government to working with families with complex needs at an earlier point in order to

---

Box 2.2 Wellbeing goals in Wales (Welsh Government 2015b)

A prosperous Wales: An innovative, productive and low carbon society which recognises the limits of the global environment and therefore uses resources efficiently and proportionately (including acting on climate change); and which develops a skilled and well-educated population in an economy which generates wealth and provides employment opportunities, allowing people to take advantage of the wealth generated through securing decent work.

A resilient Wales: A nation which maintains and enhances a biodiverse natural environment with healthy functioning ecosystems that support social, economic and ecological resilience and the capacity to adapt to change (for example climate change).

A healthier Wales A society in which people's physical and mental wellbeing is maximised and in which choices and behaviours that benefit future health are understood.

A more equal Wales: A society that enables people to fulfil their potential no matter what their background or circumstances (including their socio-economic background and circumstances).

A Wales of cohesive communities: Attractive, viable, safe and well-connected communities.

A Wales of vibrant culture and thriving Welsh language: A society that promotes and protects culture, heritage and the Welsh language, and which encourages people to participate in the arts and sports and recreation.

A globally responsible Wales: A nation which, when doing anything to improve the economic, social, environmental and cultural wellbeing of Wales, takes account of whether doing such a thing may make a positive contribution to global wellbeing.

---

safeguard children and prevent the breakdown of their relationships. Each local authority has a duty to establish (either by itself or in partnership with other Local Authorities) an Integrated Family Support Board. These oversee and support the work of the Integrated Family Support Team in their areas. As a minimum the teams comprise a core of five highly skilled staff which represent the following professions – nursing, social work, health visiting, with at least one being a consultant social worker. The child's usual social worker remains accountable for the case and works closely with the Integrated Family Support Team in supporting the family. The teams work in two phases – an initial intensive intervention of around four to six weeks, and a longer second phase to maintain the family plan of around 12 months. In Phase One an identified team member works on a 'one to one' basis with the family, helping each family member to diagnose their problems, establish goals to improve their behaviour and come to the mutually agreed Family Plan that will document how to achieve those goals. The teams also facilitate the families' access to wider services such as substance misuse services, housing services, education and probation services to enable change to be sustained.

The Welsh Government outlined its vision for mental health services in Together for Mental Health – A Mental Health and Wellbeing Strategy for Wales in 2012 (Welsh Government 2012). This followed previous reforms which had sought to improve integrated care for people with mental problems but had not achieved this consistently in practice. For example, the Welsh Audit Office report in 2005 that stated that there was 'scope for greater integration and coordination of adult mental health services across different agencies and care sectors' (Welsh Audit Office 2005, p7). The follow-on audit in 2011 suggests there was a continued need to improve collaboration between mental health services. For example, 'in some parts of Wales, there are issues with team membership, the extent of integration between health and social care, and coordination with other specialist services such as drug and alcohol services, criminal justice, and housing' (Welsh Audit Office 2011, p9). The report also highlighted that many people accessing services still did not have a single care plan with coordinated support. This was put down partly to difficulties in the planning of services with too many national directives and variable effectiveness of local strategic groups.

Together for Mental Health seeks to improve mental wellbeing across people's life course and therefore includes direction for services for children, working age adults and older people. It seeks to take an approach based on people's human rights, and sets out a series of high and lower level outcomes to be realised by 2022. Implementation of the strategy is coordinated in the seven Health Board areas by Local Partnerships. These have senior representation from health, social care, housing, education and criminal justice sectors. There is also representation of people with lived experience and from the voluntary and community sector. The local arrangements were mirrored by a National Mental Health Partnership Board which monitors implementation across the country. Better integration was seen as vital component of achieving the expected outcomes, e.g. (Welsh Government 2013):

Partner agencies will be expected to jointly plan and provide integrated services and environments to meet the needs of those with mental health problems in a person-centred approach (p19)

Service planners will be asked to review care pathways with service users to make sure they are seamless (p19)

Mental health services and physical health services must work together to make sure that the physical health needs of people with mental illnesses are met (p20)

Youth justice services and CAMHS need to develop links with police and other appropriate criminal justice agencies (p21)

Improving the mental health for people of all ages therefore needs all Government departments, public services, voluntary and independent sectors to work together (p29)

Better integration within mental health services in Wales had previously been embedded in law through the Mental Health (Wales) Measure 2010 (Mental Health Wales 2018). This sought to ensure that mental health care was predominantly provided in primary care settings such as general practice, and that people who do receive a specialist mental health service experience coordinated services. This will be achieved through people being actively engaged in the development of their individual and recovery focused Care and Treatment Plan, and through all people who access secondary health care services being appointed a Care Coordinator. The Mental Health Strategy adopted implementation of the Mental Health Measure within its work.

During 2017 and 2018 an independent review of health and social care in Wales was commissioned by the Cabinet Secretary for Health, Well-being and Sport. With cross-party support, a group of international experts were asked to make recommendations on how to improve outcomes, reduce existing inequalities and enable the systems to be sustainable for the next ten years. The interim review, published in 2017, noted that 'seamless integration between all parts of the system was described as the exception, not the rule' (Welsh Government 2017, p30). It describes many older people as not being discharged swiftly from hospital when they are ready to move on to a more community-based setting and that this puts them potentially at risk. Despite the legislation and policy expectation of more integrated planning of services, the interim report highlights that those tasked with delivering this in practice were frustrated by 'separate governance, accountability, regulatory and financial systems of health and social care' (ibid., p54). Alongside the parliamentary review was a separate inquiry by the Welsh Assembly into the work of primary care clusters (National Assembly for Wales 2017). Sixty-four clusters had been developed across Wales to facilitate better planning and delivery of primary care services for populations of 30,000 to 50,000. With the help of the Local Health Board this should include engagement with other services in their cluster area, including social care. The inquiry discovered considerable variation in the range of professionals within clusters and in the degree of involvement of social care. It did though report than there was a slow but steady trend for clusters to move from being largely focused on general practice to a broader set of neighbourhood connections (Box 2.3).

Box 2.3 Neighbourhood clusters in Gwent (ABUHB 2017)

Neighbourhood Cluster Networks in Gwent comprise primary care, health and social care community providers, public health professionals and representatives of the third sector. The networks are largely led by general practitioners, but one is led by a Public Health Specialist and another by a Senior Nurse. The following principles are used to underpin the development and delivery work of the Networks:

- To be mechanisms to enable change and promote engagement;
- To facilitate collaboration across the Health Board, Local Authorities, Public Health Wales, Third Sector, Housing and local communities;
- To facilitate the integration of services;
- To enable a changed workforce skill mix and estate to support more delivery in primary care.

By 2017, £1.1 million was delegated to the Network Leads. They determined locally their priorities for this expenditure and these have included a range of workforce developments, including the appointment of pharmacists, physiotherapists and practice-based social workers. The Networks collaborated around local shared resources, such as the purchase of the Dementia Road Map and in the developing of new services such as Anticipatory Care Planning in Care Homes.

Welsh Councils have an important role in coordinating contributions from different partners against a common vision (in this case for older people). However, in 2015 it was reported that these partners do not recognise how councils are seeking to take up this leadership role (Welsh Audit Office 2015). Welsh Government's Strategy for Older People 2008–13 introduced (and initially funded) older people's strategy coordinators within each local authority. Whilst initially these roles were seen as effectively engaging with local older people and providing strategic momentum, the Welsh Audit Office found in 2015 that postholders had much less capacity to undertake this alongside other responsibilities (ibid.). The Audit Office found it difficult to report on the impact of the Intermediate Care Fund in pump-priming sustainable preventative services due to weaknesses in the reporting and evaluation process. Insufficient data to understand more integrated approaches across sectors was highlighted in relation to other preventative services. Despite these reports of limitations in leadership and data, a review of delayed-transfers-of-care in Cardiff & Vale (at that time one of the areas with most pressure on this transition) suggested that that there was good collaboration between partners. Crucially, all agencies were described as being focused on how to work together and with older people to support their independence (Welsh Audit Office 2016).

Following the Parliamentary review, a new strategy for health and social care in Wales was launched in 2018. Once again this will have integrated care at its heart and will seek to build upon previous initiatives rather than go in a different direction – 'speed up change, not to go in a different direction … through local innovation which feeds through to new models of seamless health and social care' (Welsh Government 2018c, p2). The plan is based on five main principles – that health and social care systems will work together, that services will be shifted out of hospital to communities, there will be improved measurement of what matters to people, greater use of technology and making Wales a better place to work. A £100 million Transformation Fund has been launched to support 'time limited' projects that could inform the introduction of new models across the country. For example, Cwmtawe Cluster Project in West Wales will include a community hub through which people can access information on local services, joint health and social care teams, link workers and new IT systems within primary care.

There are many more policies in each of the home nations that seek to improve integrated care for specific populations and/ or address particular problems. Research a policy that is relevant to your own area of interest but which you do not know that much about. How do its objectives and elements compare with those which have been discussed in this chapter? Are there comparable polices in the other home nations?

Northern Ireland

a new model for the delivery of integrated health and social care services focused on prevention initiatives and earlier interventions, and on promoting health and wellbeing ... more services should be provided in the community, closer to people's homes where possible and that there should be more personalised care ... We must ensure that we keep our service users and patients at the front and centre of this process and ensure provision of safe, sustainable, resilient and effective services provided in the right place at the right time, by the right people.

(Minister for Health, Social Services and Public Safety 2011)

Unlike the other home nations, Northern Ireland has a long history of health and social care being planned and delivered through single organisations. This was instigated in 1972 as a means to enable stakeholders to 'work together towards a common goal of meeting the total needs of individuals, families and communities' (Government of Northern Ireland 1969). The Health and Social Care (Reform) Act (Northern Ireland) 2009 led to the introduction of the Health and Social Care Board as a single commissioning body for the whole of Northern Ireland. The Board oversees allocation of resources and performance management of five Health and Social Care Trusts. It also directly manages contracts with primary care services such as general practice, opticians and community pharmacists. The trusts deliver most of the other health care services, social work services and many direct social care services. A sixth trust provides ambulance services. In 2016 the Health Minister within the Northern Ireland Assembly announced that the Health and Social Care Board would be abolished to reduce bureaucracy. Its functions were to be absorbed into central government but by 2018 this had not yet been implemented.

Unlike other parts of the UK, social workers in Northern Ireland are employed mainly by Health and Social Care Trusts. Within these trusts, social workers are often based within multidisciplinary teams in which the manager is not from a social work background. Concerns have been raised from the profession that the 'consequence of models designed to deliver better inter-professional working has been a much diminished professional social work identity' (NIASW 2014, p4). A 10-year national strategy for social work published in 2012 set out to help consolidate social work's status within organisations dominated by health care professions. This promoted its particular expertise and contribution, and emphasised the responsibilities of employers to ensure that there was ongoing professional development and support for social workers (DHSSPS 2012). A review of the strategy in 2016 suggested that this vision of social work had not yet been widely adopted and there were challenges with implementation. There had therefore not been as much progress as hoped in strengthening professional practise of social work and thereby improving the lives of vulnerable people (DHSSPS 2016a).

The Minister for Health, Social Services and Public Safety announced a major review of the health and social care services in 2011. The Transforming Your Care review considered health and social care services across the whole population and life-course, and included population health as well as the delivery of direct care and support. The review team engaged widely with the public, with professionals and with other stakeholders. As well as the demographic challenges outlined above, the review team was concerned about continuing inequalities. It suggested that addressing these would 'need meaningful partnerships and a common agenda to be developed with local government, housing, education, the environment, and our local communities' (DHSSPS 2011). The review's initial setting out of the current state of play concluded that there was 'an opportunity to consider a more integrated model for the HSC system that allows us to deliver an excellent health and social care service to the population of Northern Ireland' (ibid., p36). It proposed that in future health and care services should be more explicitly organised around the individual concerned rather than organisational functions.

Central to developing the more integrated and community-based working envisaged under Transforming Your Care was the introduction of Integrated Care Partnerships (Birrell & Heenan 2014). There are 17 such partnerships which are each responsible for a population of around 100,000 people. The vision is that they will be 'multi-sector collaborative networks of health and social care providers that come together to respond innovatively to the assessed care needs of local communities' (Health & Social Board 2013, p2). Their purpose is to work at both strategic and patient levels (see Box 2.4) to improve outcomes for individuals and families through constructively challenging current practice and introducing innovative ways of working. It was envisaged that this would include the shifting of resources from hospital settings to primary and community provision. Their initial focus was on populations with identified health and social care needs such as older people, those with long-term conditions or those who require palliative care. They individually negotiate with their local Health and Social Care Trust as to how their performance is to be measured and also provide regular updates on progress to a regional implementation team.

Each partnership is constituted as a committee of 14 members that is outside of the other health and social care structures. The stakeholder groups that have to represented in the membership are mandated, for example two pharmacists and two people with lived experience (see Box 2.5). The members decide on who will be the chair and (in 2014) the majority of chairs were general practitioners (Birrell & Heenan 2014).

**Box 2.4 Levels of work of Integrated Care Partnerships
(Birrell & Heenan 2014)**

Strand 1: Strategic Level – Local application of fully integrated, Commissioner-approved care pathways to ensure coordinated and effective delivery; evaluation of local effectiveness of existing care pathways with a view to service improvement; risk stratification of a defined population of service users; contribution to comparative benchmarking between ICPs and the sharing of best practice.

Strand 2: Patient level – agreeing the processes for anonymised casework: care planning; case reviews of patients at significant risk of poor outcomes relating to the condition under consideration, to include the promotion of self-care and independence; improvement in control and prevention of inappropriate acute admission and information sharing.

**Box 2.5 Integrated Care Partnership membership
(DHSSPS 2016b)**

Four members from the local Trust (hospital and community staff, to include a medical specialist, a nurse, an AHP and social worker)
One member from the NI Ambulance Service
One member from the voluntary sector
One member from the community sector
Two service user/carer representatives
Two general practitioners
Two community pharmacists
One Council representative

The limited research activity of integration within Northern Ireland is surprising when it provides such a unique governance structure within the United Kingdom (Heenan & Birrell 2018). There is therefore little evidence to understand how commissioning and delivering health and social care services through similar bodies has impacted on quality and efficiency. An expert panel led by Professor Bengoa considered the evidence that was available (DHSSPS 2016b). They concluded that 'health and social care are not working together as effectively as they might. If they were, there would be better outcomes and reduced waste' (ibid., p37). It goes on to state that transforming the health and care system 'will require a great deal more work on how the system plans, funds and purchases care across acute care, general practice and community health, and social care provided by statutory, independent and community, voluntary and charitable providers' (p45). Integrated Care Partnerships have been criticised as they must only contain one social work representative but two from pharmacy and general practitioners. In total they must contain eight members from a health background (Birrell & Heenan 2014). Their description as 'networks' has also been questioned as there is a limited number of members with a formal (rather than emergent) set of objectives (ibid.). The impact report published in 2016 does though report that 'integrated services are now being delivered across a number of localities and condition areas leading to positive patient experiences' (Health & Social Care Board 2016, p26).

England

Regardless of whether our discussions were focussed on the issue of public accountability and patient involvement, competition and choice or clinical advice and leadership, concerns around integration came up time and time again. The importance of collaboration and integration between different care sectors and care settings are, therefore, strong themes in each of the separate work stream reports.

(NHS Future Forum 2011, p20)

The initial proposals by the Conservative–Liberal Democratic Coalition government in 2010 did not have a particular emphasis on integrated care. The focus was on the establishment of GP-led Clinical Commissioning Groups to plan and purchase health services and help to increase competitive pressures within the NHS. The transfer of public health responsibilities to local government and the creation of Health and Well-being Boards (see below) were the main developments relevant to integrated care. Integration became a greater priority following the NHS Future Forum. This was a national body set up to consult on the proposed changes as the legislation was progressing through parliament. Hearing from many stakeholders that the proposed reforms could create greater fragmentation, the Forum focusing a specific strand of its work on 'integrated care' emphasising that this was crucial to responding to the challenges facing both health and social care (see quote above).

The Forum had made a number of detailed recommendations on how to support integrated care which were broadly accepted by the Coalition (NHS Future Forum 2012). A subsequent vision for integrated care was expressed by the National Collaboration for Integrated Care and Support in 2013. This was an umbrella group comprising key central governmental bodies, the Associations of Directors of Children's Services and Adult Social Services, the Local Government Association and National Voices. As well as adopting the person-centred narrative, the Collaboration identified that the purpose of integration was to achieve three purposes (the Triple Aims) – outcomes for individuals, effective use of resources and addressing health inequalities. The final Health and Social Care Act 2012 included a 'duty to integrate' placed on NHS England, Monitor and CCGs and Health and Wellbeing Boards, with similar provision for local authority adult social care in the 2014 Care Act. The NHS Five Year Forward View highlighted the need for a more integrated and holistic approach to respond to the ongoing care needs of patients with long-term health conditions if the NHS was going to address the predicted £30 billion shortfall by 2020–12 (NHSE 2014). The Spending

Review and Autumn Statement 2015 set out an aim for health and social care to be integrated across England by 2020 (HM Treasury 2015). To monitor progress a scorecard of integration will be developed which combines user experience, financial performance and outcome metrics. The Next Steps on the Five Year Forward View (NHSE 2017) confirmed the commitment to 'move towards the greatest integrated health system of any western country' (p31).

Each upper tier/unitary local authority was required to develop a Health and Wellbeing Board by April 2013 (Coleman et al. 2016). These have a legal duty to promote integrated care including the deployment of the Better Care Fund (see below). Run as sub-committees of the local authority, there is specified requirement for a minimum core membership and each Board can then choose to recruit additional members. The core membership must include:

- at least one nominated councillor of the local authority
- the director of adult social services for the local authority
- the director of children's services for the local authority
- the director of public health for the local authority
- a representative of the local HealthWatch organisation
- a representative of each relevant commissioning group.

The primary task of Health and Wellbeing Boards is to undertake a joint strategic needs assessment for the local population. This should set out the needs of their local population and lead to an agreed joint health and wellbeing strategy to respond to these needs. Local commissioning plans for health, social care and public health should then all reflect the intent of this strategy. Boards do not hold a budget as such, and their impact is essentially through providing strategic leadership and encouraging more collaborative working across the system.

In April 2015, the Department of Health and the Department for Communities and Local Government, NHS England and the Local Government Association launched the Better Care Fund (Miller & Glasby 2016). The main aim of the Better Care Fund was to drive the transformation of local services to ensure that people receive better and more integrated care and support. This would be achieved principally by reducing demand for hospital services. The Fund requires local health bodies and local authorities in each Health and Wellbeing Board area to pool funding. This amounted to a minimum of £3.8 billion in 2015–16 and £3.9 billion in 2016–17 across England. In 2015–16, the £3.8 billion pooled fund comprised the existing £1.1 billion transfer from the NHS to adult social care, a further £1.9 billion of NHS funding transferred from NHS budgets to the pool, £130 million carers' breaks funding, £300 million reablement funding and £354 million capital funding (including £220 million Disabled Facilities Grant). Local bodies must produce joint plans for integrating services and reducing pressure on hospitals, and agree targets against a set of national performance metrics. These plans are submitted to central government to show how they will use their pooled budget to meet a series of national conditions. Many areas chose to go beyond the minimum pooled funding requirements, resulting in a total of £5.3 billion being pooled in 2015–16 and £5.8 billion in 2016–17.

To help understand how to overcome challenges to integration at 'pace and scale', the National Collaboration for Integrated Care and Support (2013) announced a series of 'local integration pioneers' to test out new approaches to delivery and commissioning (Erens et al. 2016). Expressions of interest from the 'most ambitious and visionary' local areas were sought in May 2013. Pioneers were required to 'articulate a clear vision of their own innovative approaches to integrated care and support, including how they will utilise the Narrative developed by National Voices' and 'present fully developed plans for whole system integration, encompassing health, social care and public health, other public services and the community and voluntary sector, as appropriate'. Successful candidates would be given access to expertise, support and constructive challenge from a range of national and international experts. A total of 25 Pioneer sites were selected and launched in two waves: 14 in November 2013 and 11 in January 2015. They have tended to concentrate on specific sets of interventions for older people with substantial needs; typically, multidisciplinary teams based in primary care that identify and manage patients at risk of hospital admission.

The NHS Five Year Forward View introduced a number of new care models with an emphasis on integrated care between acute and primary care, and between health and social care (NHS England 2016). The Vanguard programme was launched in 2015 to support fifty local sites test out the implementation of these new models (Box 2.6). Similar to the Pioneer programme, the Vanguards received support, profile and networking opportunities. Unlike the Pioneers, they also received significant investment of £329 million between 2015 and 2018 with an additional £80 million being spent on wider support and monitoring of the Vanguards. Learning from the Vanguard programme has been summarise through a series of leaning guides. There is also a national evaluation underway and a plan to synthesise the local evaluations completed by each of the Vanguard sites.

Box 2.6 New care models in England

Multispecialty community providers (fourteen sites): expanding GP practices; bringing in nurses, community health services and hospital specialists to provide integrated out-of-hospital care, shifting the majority of consultations and ambulatory care out of hospitals.

Primary and acute care systems (nine sites): hospital and primary care providers come together to provide NHS list-based GP and hospital services, together with mental health and community care services.

Enhanced health in care homes (six sites): care homes and local authority social services departments work together to develop new shared care models and support. This covers medical and medication reviews and rehabilitation services.

Urgent and emergency care (eight sites) Creating new approaches to improve coordination of services and reduce pressure on accident and emergency departments.

The NHS planning guidance in December 2015 set out a requirement for local areas to develop health and social care partnerships to lead the implementation of the Five Year Forward View (NHSE 2015). These would be locally designed around 44 'footprints'. The Sustainability and Transformation partnerships were asked to estimate the funding gap of their footprint and jointly develop a plan to address this gap. These plans were published by December 2016. A new national fund was created in 2016–17 to support the transformation process (although in practice much of this has been diverted to maintaining the current financial position of NHS providers). In some areas, Sustainability and Transformation Partnerships have dovetailed with devolution of power and/or funding from central government. Most notably this relates to Greater Manchester in which the ten local authorities and matching clinical commissioning groups have taken local control of health and social care budgets.

The focus then shifted from the original Sustainability and Transformation *Plans* and more on the *Partnerships*. Partnerships that made good progress could apply for the status of 'integrated care system' (ICS) (NHSE 2018). An ICS would have greater autonomy over how they deploy available funding and a collective responsibility for responding to any challenges of quality within their health and care system. By August 2018 fourteen areas had been designated as ICSs. The Ten Year Plan launched in 2019 committed England to establishing an ICS in every locality.

Alongside Sustainability and Transformation Partnerships have been the creation of Transforming Care Partnerships (LGA et al. 2015a). These were introduced as part of the Transforming Care programme to improve local support for people with a learning disability and/or autism and behaviour that challenges. Some progress had been made following the tragic events at Winterbourne View through initiatives such as a national concordant between the main providers and the introduction of local registers of people with such need. By 2014 there was thought to be still over 3000 people being treated in assessment and treatment facilities and they had an average length of stay of over 17 years. A commitment was therefore made to reduce the number of people within in-patient facilities by 50 per cent by 2019. The programme involves the implementation of a national service model which set out the support which people and their families would need to remain in their community. Multi-agency Care and Treatment Reviews were now to be completed in respect of anyone either already in hospital or at risk of being admitted, with a named care coordinator being identified. The Transforming Care Partnerships brought together local commissioners, providers and specialist commissioners of forensic services to plan how to implement the model for adults and children in their local areas. This included developing pooled budgets across health and social care to reduce arguments about funding responsibilities and enable more joined up planning.

In 2018 there were a series of reports published by national bodies regarding progress with integrated between health and social care. This included the Care Quality Commission (2018), the National Audit Office (2018) and the House of Commons Health and Social Care Committee (2018). These highlighted that there had been progress in some local areas in addressing long-standing barriers to health and social care integration. Sustainability and Transformation Partnerships were enabling local authorities and NHS organisations to move beyond their traditional geographic boundaries to focus instead on the 'place' that makes most sense for the services concerned. For example, neighbourhoods of between 30,000 and 50,000 people were commonly being considered for integration around primary care. Progress has been made in regard to improved information sharing through local areas developing agreements between local authorities, hospitals and primary care services. More preventative approaches to address social determinants of poor health were being introduced in many areas such as social prescribing.

The reports conclude however that despite such progress there is still a long way before the potential benefits of integrated care are realised. Funding pressures were resulting in some health and social care services blaming each other for their difficulties in maintaining their financial viability. This built on previous disagreements in local areas about how people with continuing health care needs should have their packages of support funded. The need to achieve short-term savings also detracted some areas from focusing on long-term transformation of services. Uncertainty about the future of social care funding (due for a review in 2018 which was then delayed) further prevented long-term planning. The priorities of national bodies were seen to sometimes be competing and lacking the coherence necessary for local organisations to feel confident in embracing new ways of working. The legal duty on commissioners to not be anti-competitive was causing uncertainty with legal challenges on the introduction of alliance contracts across providers. National payment rules such as the set tariff through which hospitals are paid for each patient seen or treated encouraged hospitals to increase their activity rather than work with other partners to support more care in the community.

Looking across the four home nations summarise the main elements of their approaches to making care more integrated. If you can, try to conceptualise them as a type of intervention (e.g. funding, partnership body, pathway). Now compare these between the countries – what is similar, and what is different?

Further resources

Journal of Integrated Care www.emeraldinsight.com/journal/jica

This is the United Kingdom's leading journal looking at practice, policy and the research of integrated care. It includes contributions from all of the home nations.

King's Fund www.kingsfund.org.uk

The King's Fund is an independent charity working to improve health and health care in the United Kingdom. The organisation helps to shape policy and practice through research and analysis; develops individuals, teams and organisations; promotes understanding of the health and social care system; and brings people together to learn, share knowledge and debate. The organisation's on-line resources include video clips of key speakers leading UK and international integrated care projects.

Local Government Representative Bodies England: www.local.gov.uk **Northern Ireland**: www.nilga.org **Scotland**: www.cosla.gov.uk **Wales**: www.wlga.gov.uk

These represent the views and interests of local government across policy issues including integrated care. This includes briefings on policy and good practice examples.

Nuffield Trust www.nuffieldtrust.org.uk

The Nuffield Trust is an independent think tank. It aims to improve the quality of health and social care in the UK by providing evidence-based research and policy analysis and informing and generating debate.

Scottish Parliament Information Centre www.parliament.scot/parliamentarybusiness/research.aspx

The Scottish Parliament Information Centre (SPICe) produces research briefings and fact sheets on policy developments and the underpinning evidence.

References

ABUHB. (2017). *Health, Social Care and Sport Committee's inquiry into primary care*. Available at: http://senedd.assembly.wales/

documents/s59989/PC%2043%20Aneurin%20Bevan%20Univer
sity%20Health%20Board.html?CT=2 (downloaded 04.11.2018)

Audit Scotland. (2015). Health and social care integration. Available at: www.audit-scotland.gov.uk/uploads/docs/report/2015/nr_151203_health_socialcare.pdf (downloaded 04.11.2018)

Audit Scotland. (2016). Social work in Scotland. Available at: www.audit-scotland.gov.uk/report/social-work-in-scotland (downloaded 04.11.2018)

Birrell, D., & Heenan, D. (2014). Integrated Care Partnerships in Northern Ireland: added value or added bureaucracy? *Journal of Integrated Care*, 22(5/6), 197–207.

Brock, J., & Everingham, S. (2018). *Integrated children's services in Scotland: practice and leadership*. Available at: https://childreninscotland.org.uk/wp-content/uploads/2018/06/Integrated-Children%E2%80%99s-Services-in-Scotland-Practice-and-Leadership.pdf (downloaded 04.11.2018)

Burgess, L. (2016). *SPICe briefing: integration of health and social care*. Available at: www.parliament.scot/ResearchBriefingsAndFactsheets/S5/SB_16-70_Integration_of_Health_and_Social_Care.pdf (downloaded 04.11.2018)

Care Quality Commission. (2018). *Beyond barriers. How older people move between health and social care in England*. Available at: www.cqc.org.uk/publications/themed-work/beyond-barriers-how-older-people-move-between-health-care-england (downloaded 05.11.2018)

Coleman, A., Dhesi, S., & Peckham, S. (2016). Health and Well-being Boards: the new system stewards. In Exworthy, M., Mannion, R., & Powell, M. (eds.). *Dismantling the NHS: evaluating the impact of health reform*. Bristol: Policy Press. 279–300.

Department of Health, Social Services & Public Safety. (2011). Transforming your care: a review of health and social care in Northern Ireland. Available at: www.health-ni.gov.uk/topics/health-policy/transforming-your-care (downloaded 04.11.2018)

Department of Health, Social Services & Public Safety. (2012). *Improving and safeguarding social wellbeing: a strategy for* social work in Northern Ireland 2012–2022*. Available at: www. health-ni.gov.uk/publications/improving-and-safeguarding-social-wellbeing-strategy-social-work-northern-ireland   (downloaded 04.11.2018)

Department of Health, Social Services & Public Safety. (2016a). *Improving and safeguarding social wellbeing*. Available at: www. health-ni.gov.uk/sites/default/files/publications/health/Putting% 20Improvement%20at%20the%20Heart%20of%20Social% 20Work.pdf

Department of Health, Social Services & Public Safety. (2016b). *Systems, not structures – changing health and social care – full report*. Available at: www.health-ni.gov.uk/publications/systems-not-structures-changing-health-and-social-care-full-report (downloaded 05.11.2018)

Erens, B., Wistow, G., Mounier-Jack, S., Douglas, N., Jones, L., Manacorda, T., Durand, M.A., & Mays, N. (2016). Early findings from the evaluation of the integrated care and support pioneers in England. *Journal of Integrated Care*, 25(3), 137–149.

Government of Northern Ireland. (1969). *The administrative structure of health and personal social services in Northern Ireland*. Belfast: HMSO. In Heenan, D. & Birrell, D. (2018) *The integration of health and social care in the UK*. London: Palgrave.

Health & Social Care Board. (2013). *Integrated care partnerships: policy implementation framework*. Available at: www. hscboard.hscni.net/download/PUBLICATIONS/icps/publica tions/ICP-Policy-Implementation-Framework.pdf   (downloaded 05.11.2018)

Health & Social Care Board. (2016). *Integrated Care Partnerships: interim impact report*. Available at: www.hscboard.hscni.net/ download/PUBLICATIONS/icps/publications/icp-impact-report-aug-2016.pdf (downloaded 05.11.2018)

Heenan, D., & Birrell, D. (2018). *The integration of health and social care in the UK*. London: Palgrave.

HM Treasury. (2015). *Spending review and autumn statement 2015*. Available at: https://assets.publishing.service.gov.uk/govern ment/uploads/system/uploads/attachment_data/file/479749/

52229_Blue_Book_PU1865_Web_Accessible.pdf   (downloaded 05.11.2018)

House of Commons Health & Social Care Committee. (2018). *Integrated care: organisations, partnerships and systems*. Available at: www.parliament.uk/business/committees/committees-a-z/commons-select/health-committee/inquiries/parliament-2017/inquiry4/(downloaded 05.11.2018)

Joint Improvement Team. (2012). *Maximising recovery, promoting independence: an intermediate care framework for Scotland*. Available at: www2.gov.scot/Publications/2012/07/1181 (downloaded 04.11.2018)

Kidner, C. (2013). *SPICe briefing. Children and Young People (Scotland) Bill*. Available at: http://dera.ioe.ac.uk/18467/1/SB_13-38.pdf (downloaded 04.11.2018)

LGA, ADASS & NHSE. (2015a). *Building the right support*. Available at: www.england.nhs.uk/wp-content/uploads/2015/10/ld-nat-imp-plan-oct15.pdf (downloaded 05.11.2018)

LGA, ADASS & NHSE. (2015b). *Supporting people with a learning disability and/or autism who display behaviour that challenges, including those with a mental health condition*. Available at: www.england.nhs.uk/wp-content/uploads/2015/10/service-model-291015.pdf (downloaded 05.11.2018)

Mental Health Wales. (2018). *Mental Health Measure*. Available at: www.mentalhealthwales.net/mental-health-measure/ (downloaded 04.11.2018)

Miller, R., & Glasby, J. (2016). 'Much ado about nothing'? Pursuing the 'holy grail' of health and social care integration under the Coalition. In Exworthy, M., Mannion, R., & Powell, M. (eds.). *Dismantling the NHS: evaluating the impact of health reform*. Bristol: Policy Press. 171-190.

Minister for Health, Social Services and Public Safety. (2011). *About Transforming Your Care*. Available at: www.transformingyourcare.hscni.net/about/ (downloaded 04.11.2018)

National Assembly for Wales. (2017). *Health Social Care and Sport Committee inquiry into primary care: clusters*. Available at:

www.assembly.wales/laid%20documents/cr-ld11226/cr-ld 11226-e.pdf (downloaded 04.11.2018)

National Audit Office. (2018). *Developing new care models through NHS Vanguards*. Available at: www.nao.org.uk/report/developing-new-care-models-through-nhs-vanguards/ (downloaded 05.11. 2018)

National Collaboration for Integrated Care. (2013). *Integrated care and support: our shared commitment*. Available at: www.gov.uk/government/publications/integrated-care (downloaded 05.11. 2018)

NHS England. (2016). New care models: Vanguards: developing a blueprint for the future of NHS and care services. Available at: www.england.nhs.uk/wp-content/uploads/2015/11/new_care_models.pdf (downloaded 05.11.2018)

NHS Future Forum. (2011). *Summary report on proposed changes to the NHS*. Available at: https://assets.publishing.service.gov.uk /government/uploads/system/uploads/attachment_data/file/ 213748/dh_127540.pdf (downloaded 05.11.2018)

NHS Future Forum. (2012). *Integration: a report from the NHS Future Forum*. Available at: www.gov.uk/government/publications/nhs-future-forum-recommendations-to-government-second-phase (downloaded 05.11.2018)

NHSE. (2014) *Five Year Forward View*. Available at: www .england.nhs.uk/wp-content/uploads/2014/10/5yfv-web.pdf (downloaded 05.11.2018)

NHSE. (2015). *Delivering the Forward View: NHS planning guidance 2016/17 – 2020/21*. Available at: www.england.nhs.uk/wp-content/uploads/2015/12/planning-guid-16-17-20-21.pdf (down-loaded 05.11.2018)

NHSE. (2017). *Next steps on the NHS Five Year Forward View*. Available at: www.england.nhs.uk/wp-content/uploads/2017/03/ NEXT-STEPS-ON-THE-NHS-FIVE-YEAR-FORWARD-VIEW.pdf (downloaded 05.11.2018)

NHSE. (2018). *Integrated care systems*. Available at: www. england.nhs.uk/integratedcare/integrated-care-systems/ (down-loaded 05.11.2018)

Northern Ireland Association of Social Workers. (2014). *A blueprint for change for adult services social work in Northern Ireland.* Available at: www.basw.co.uk/resources/blueprint-change-adult-services-social-work-northern-ireland (downloaded 04.11.2018)

Powys Regional Partnership Board. (2018). *Health and care strategy 2017–2027.* Available at: file:///C:/Users/millerrs/Downloads/180328_Delivering_the_Vision_Full_documentv9%20(1).pdf

Scottish Government. (2015). *National health and wellbeing outcomes.* Available at: www.gov.scot/Resource/0047/00470219.pdf. (downloaded 04.11.2018)

Scottish Government. (2018). Intermediate care. Available at: www.gov.scot/Topics/Health/Support-Social-Care/Independent-Living/Intermediate-Care (downloaded 04.11.2018)

Scottish Parliament. (2013). *Public Bodies (Joint Working) (Scotland) Bill – explanatory notes.* Available at: www.parliament.scot/S4_Bills/Public%20Bodies%20(Joint%20Working)%20(Scotland)%20Bill/b32s4-introd-en.pdf (downloaded 04.11.2018)

Welsh Audit Office. (2005). *Adult mental health services in Wales: a baseline review of service provision.* Available at: www.wales.nhs.uk/documents/Adult_Mental_Health_Services_Baseline_Review.pdf (downloaded 04.11.2018)

Welsh Audit Office. (2011). *Adult mental health services follow up report.* Available at: www.audit.wales/publication/adult-mental-health-services-follow-report (downloaded 04.11.2018)

Welsh Audit Office. (2015). *Supporting the independence of older people: are councils doing enough?* Available at: www.audit.wales/system/files/publications/Independence-Older-People-2015-English.pdf (downloaded 04.11.2018)

Welsh Audit Office. (2016). *Review of delayed transfers of care – Cardiff and Vale health and social care community.* Available at: www.audit.wales/publication/review-delayed-transfers-care-cardiff-and-vale-health-and-social-care-community (downloaded 04.11.2018)

Welsh Government. (2012). *Together for Mental Health: a strategy for mental health and wellbeing in Wales.* Available at: https://

gov.wales/topics/health/nhswales/mental-health-services/policy/
strategy/?lang=en (downloaded 04.11.2018)

Welsh Government. (2013). *Together for Mental Health: a strategy
for mental health and wellbeing in Wales. A summary*. Available
at: https://gov.wales/topics/health/nhswales/mental-health-
services/policy/strategy/?lang=en (downloaded 04.11.2018)

Welsh Government. (2015a). *Social Services and Well-being
(Wales) Act 2014: part 9 statutory guidance (partnership arrangements)*. Available at: https://socialcare.wales/research-and-data/
research-on-care-finder/social-services-and-well-being-wales-
act-2014-part-9-statutory-guidance-partnership-arrangements
(downloaded 04.11.2018)

Welsh Government. (2015b). *Well-being of Future Generations
(Wales) Act 2015: the essentials*. Available at: https://gov.wales/
topics/people-and-communities/people/future-generations-act/
?lang=en (downloaded 04.11.2018)

Welsh Government. (2017). *Parliamentary review of health and social
care in Wales. Interim report*. Available at: https://beta.gov.wales/
sites/default/files/publications/2017-07/170714-review-interim-
report-en.pdf (downloaded 04.11.2018)

Welsh Government. (2018a). *£50m fund to deliver joined-up care
closer to home*. Available at: https://gov.wales/newsroom/health-
and-social-services/2018/fund/?lang=en (downloaded 04.11.2018)

Welsh Government. (2018b). *Integrated Care Fund guidance*. Available at: https://gov.wales/topics/health/socialcare/working/icf/?
lang=en (downloaded 04.11.2018)

Welsh Government. (2018c). *A healthier Wales: our plan for
health and social care*. Available at: https://gov.wales/docs/
dhss/publications/180608healthier-wales-mainen.pdf   (downloaded 08.11.2018)

3 Theories to understand integrated care

It can be difficult to make sense of the many factors that result in people not receiving integrated care. Barriers can be created at all levels of a system including the practice of individual professionals, the institutional cultures of organisations and governmental policy and performance frameworks. Similarly, there are many potential approaches to address fragmented care that may need active engagement from many different participants. Trying to understand who needs to contribute what and when can seem a messy and bewildering task to those responsible for addressing identified weaknesses. Integrated care is therefore an example of a 'wicked' problem. These are problems for which no set solution can be applied. It may be possible to draw on learning from previous attempts to address something similar, but these will not be able to be copied as such. This is due to the diversity of local contexts, the ever-changing policy environment and uncertainties of how the individual professionals and leaders will respond. Complex problems are often contrasted with simple problems and complicated problems. Simple problems are ones in which a standard process can be followed to achieve similar results. Prior experience is not required as such but having expertise can increase the likelihood of success and the quality of what is produced. Processes can be improved over time with potential for adaptation to reflect individual situations and preferences. Complicated problems are ones in which there may be many components but with sufficient analysis each one can be understood and addressed. This requires high levels of expertise in the necessary fields of practice but with sufficient diversity and capacity the problems can be overcome. Common examples of these different types of problems are baking a cake (simple), sending a rocket to the moon (complicated) and raising a child (complex) (Glouberman & Zimmerman 2002).

Theories can help us to better understand integrated care in three main ways. The first is to provide a conceptual typology of what we mean by integration in different circumstances. Such clarity is important as it is common for such terms to be used loosely with little definition about what is being integrated and to what end. Furthermore, the meaning of terms can change over time so that what was applied at one point is different following changes in policy and academic thinking. For example, in the past 'integrated' was used to refer to situations in which there was a merger of two or more organisations to bring together the associated services and professionals. We would now refer to such approaches as being 'structural integration', i.e. a form of integration rather than integration itself. To add to potential confusion, in some academic fields such as business the term is still used to suggest the interweaving of organisations. The second contribution is to suggest theoretical lenses through which we can consider the interactions of the various actors and organisations. This can help us to unpick the dynamics that may result in care being fragmented and provide insight into how interventions can influence the behavior of the members of this system. No one theory will have all the answers, but if relevant they can provide analysis which will help to get under the surface of a particular situation. Finally, theories can set out models of what can be included in an integrated care programme to support a particular population to achieve the desired outcomes. These will always need local adaption and implementation will vary dependent on context and resources but they provide at least a starting point on which programmes can be developed.

Write down as many terms as you can that describe practices in which different professionals and services work together to support people and their families. Define them in a single sentence which would be understandable to people who are not voiced in 'professional' terminology. You may want to see how other people have tried to define such terms (see resources at the back).

Typologies of integration

Vertical–horizontal integration

The concepts of 'vertical' and 'horizontal' integration help to describe the relationship between the different services and professions that are being connected together around the individual or populations (Figure 3.1). *Vertical integration* denotes a progressive pathway in which the individual receives the appropriate support as their health condition or social situation deteriorates or improves. This may be provided by the same organisation or involve the individual transitioning from one organisation to another. Some steps of

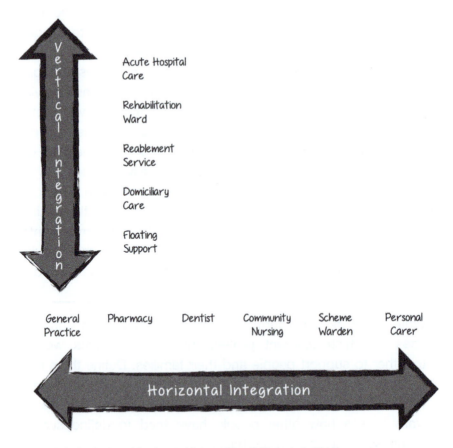

Figure 3.1 Vertical and horizontal integration (Miller et al. 2016)

the pathway may involve them receiving support in different physical locations. For example, if someone experiences a major stroke then they will commonly follow a vertically integrated pathway as set out in Figure 3.1. The first stage is often that a family member will call 999 for emergency help and the person will be visited by an ambulance. Paramedics will administer any life-saving treatment that is required and make the person safe to be transported to hospital. They will then be admitted to a stroke ward whose focus will be on responding to immediate health needs and preventing them from having further strokes. Once their condition is stabilised the focus will be on intense rehabilitation which may be provided on the stroke unit or a separate ward. The person will commonly be visited by speech, physio and occupational therapists who will work with them to recover their physical abilities. After several weeks they are likely to have regained as much of their abilities as is possible in the short term. Discharge from hospital will therefore be planned through social workers and community health professionals meeting the person and discussing their care with the hospital-based professionals. Immediate care post-discharge may be provided through a reablement service. This will provide intensive home support that aims to enable people to regain their independent living skills. This is often with the guidance of a community-based occupational therapist and will be for a time-limited period. If on-going support is required, then the reablement service will hand over to a domiciliary care agency.

Horizontal integration denotes simultaneous joint working between different professions and services with an individual at a point in time. Rather than being delivered in a progressive sequence, these are delivered in parallel to support someone with a current health condition or with their social situation. For example, an older person with multiple health conditions who is living in sheltered housing will be interacting with numerous health and social care services. This will commonly include:

• general practice for overall coordination of their health care by the practice nurse and/or doctor;

- community pharmacy for supply of their medication;
- social work to coordinate their care package and asses the needs of family carers;
- community nursing to support with physical symptoms such as pressure sores or incontinence;
- practical support and general monitoring from the sheltered housing staff;
- personal care from a domiciliary care agency or personal assistant that they are employing through a direct payment;
- social activities and networks from a voluntary organisation or other community resource.

It is worth noting that for someone to experience integrated care there will often need to be both horizontal and vertical integration. During their rehabilitation phase the person in hospital will require input from multiple therapists as well as doctors and nurses. On discharge they may receive support from a specialist community-based stroke team as well as general health and social care services. It is also worth noting that a common flaw of vertical and horizontal integration maps is that the contribution of families and other informal networks is not included. The focus is on the need for professionals to communicate and coordinate their involvement which can miss the vital role of other supports.

Micro, meso and macro integration

A common approach to grouping elements within a welfare system is around the size and scale of their influence and responsibility. These are denoted through the use of three terms – 'micro', 'meso' and 'macro'. *Micro* is used to denote the most focused unit of concern, *macro* the broadest level and *meso* between micro and macro. So, for example, in relation to integrated care for children and young people with mental health difficulties this could be used as follows:

Micro integration: Joint working between the form teacher at school, the allocated community psychiatric nurse from the Child and Adolescent Mental Health Service, the social worker and the general practitioner. This will be focused on supporting the young person and their family in relation to the difficulties that they identify.

Meso integration: Collaboration between specialist teams and organisations who are responsible and/or work within a designated locality. The focus is understanding the experience of children and young people working in that area and how the services can better engage with each other to improve this experience. For example this could be through a community partnership between local schools, youth centres, Child and Adolescent Mental Health Services, the social work team and the police.

Macro integration: Coordination between the bodies who are responsible for the overall strategic planning to improve the mental wellbeing of children and young people within a local authority area. This will involve undertaking a joint analysis of current and future needs, mapping out the available resources including those outside of statutory publicly funded services, and developing a strategic vision and implementation programme.

The comparative scale of interest from micro being the smallest to macro as the largest is always the same. It is worth noting however that the scale implied at each level can be different – for example *meso* could be used to apply to organisational partnerships and *macro* to national or regional working. Within integrated care, there are also examples in which *micro* infers integration between professionals within a single organisation and *meso* between professionals working in different organiaations. No one use of the terms is better than another – the main issue is that the meaning in each circumstance is defined clearly.

Breadth and depth of integration

All of the agencies concerned with supporting vulnerable people and their families will have multiple connections with other services and organisations. The intensity of integration around an issue should therefore depend on their contribution to improving the wellbeing of a population or resolving a particular issue. To help visualise the levels of integration being considered it can be useful to map these out onto a graph of integration (see Figure 3.2).

Breadth of integration describes the diversity of services which are being considered within the integration programme. A narrow integration focuses on a limited number of services that work with a well-defined population. For example, this could be integration between specialist health, social care and criminal justice services

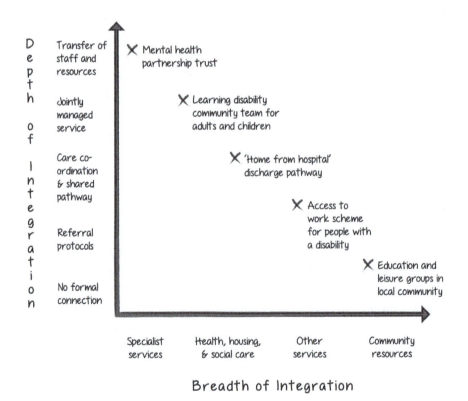

Figure 3.2 Breadth and depth of integration (Miller et al. 2016)

that support young people who have sexually offended, or integration between primary health care professionals and care home staff. A broad integration seeks to improve collaboration between a diverse range of services which work with more diffuse populations. For example, responding to the increasing rates of obesity in young people will require not only the engagement of schools and primary health care services but also sports and leisure, retail outlets and transport services

Depth of integration reflects the intensity of connection being sought and the amount of resources that are being invested in achieving this integration. For example, a referral protocol between two services that sets out what information is required, the medium through which it can be relayed and the timescales by which a response will be made will improve basic communication but not lead to a holistic discussion around the individual concerned. On the other side of the spectrum, an inter-professional team which is co-located and meets on a weekly basis to reflect on the care of the people who they support should (although see later) enable more person-centred and detailed collaboration.

The depth and breadth of integration responds to the complexity and importance of the fragmentation that has been identified. In part this is because integration is a costly business with the process of transformation requiring additional change management resources and taking up considerable time of the professionals concerned. Furthermore, most services will have to work with a range of other services and cannot be intensely integrated with all of them. For example, a social work mental health team will work on a daily basis with the specialist health psychiatric teams. It is also likely to be in regular communication with police, housing, employment and benefits agencies. It would not therefore be practicable, or desirable, to have a similar level of intensity of integration with all of these other agencies. Within strategies that are seeking to address major societal issues there will often be examples of narrow and intense, and broad and loose integration. For example, to improve rates of unemployment amongst young adults with disability we may expect to see intense and focused integration between the specialist careers advisors, special needs coordinators within colleges and adult disability teams. There will also though need to be commitment from recruitment agencies, training providers, business development agencies and employer bodies to ensure that opportunities for employment are developed and access to these coordinated.

Toolkit of integration

As reflected in the national policies of the home nations in the UK there are multiple ways in which it is possible to better integrate services around the needs of a population. Once again, no one approach to integrated care is better than another as this will depend on the problems that are being addressed and the outcomes to be achieved. It is also common and indeed necessary for different approaches to be applied simultaneously as part of an overall programme of change. Figure 3.3 provides a pictorial representation of the main approaches within the toolkit to promote integrated care.

Integration of values and vision relates to the development of a single vision of what will be achieved and the shared principles on which decisions and behaviours will be based. The benefits of such integration processes are that they can inspire professionals from different services and backgrounds to work towards a common goal. This helps to connect integration with the intrinsic motivations that lead to many people undertaking such vocations. This can result in greater willingness to engage with the connected transformation programmes including changes to their own roles. Developing shared values and vision is a central part of system leadership (see below).

Integration of system governance relates to the processes through which organisations, professions and partnerships within a system are overseen in relation to their quality, performance

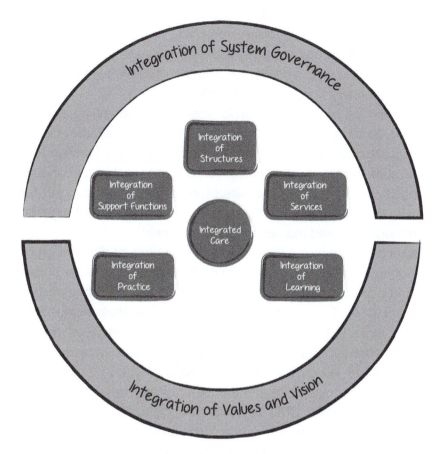

Figure 3.3 Toolkit of integration (Miller et al. 2016)

and financial health. Examples of governance processes would include inspections by an external regulator, registration require- ments for professions, financial incentives or punishments and publishing of achievement against national performance frame- works. Ensuring that the governance processes and standards for different organisations are complementary and working towards the same standards and outcomes encourages and enables organisations to work better together.

Integration of structures brings together formal institutions such as organisations and partnership bodies. This may be achieved through merging into a single entity by one organisation taking on the responsibilities (and connected resources) of another, or by organisations collectively morphing into a new undertaking. Developing formal legal agreements between organisations is another means to ensure that structurally they have an imperative to better coordinate their work.

Integration of services relates to integrating the management of staff, funding and/or other resources from separate services and in some cases organisations. This may involve the formal transfer of staff from one organisation on a permanent or secondment basis. It can also be organised through staff remaining in their current employment but their work being overseen and organised through a shared management arrangement.

Integration of practice seeks to connect the work of different professionals and services in their existing structures through introducing common pathways, shared guidelines or case management processes. The focus is not on changing their management structures but ensuring that their individual practices complement each other around the needs of the person concerned.

Integration of learning involves developing shared opportunities for professionals to undertake learning and development. This varies from short CPD sessions through to formal qualification programmes. It may include inter-professional education in which participants learn from each other as well as through the designated tutor.

Integration of support functions are what are called 'back room functions', relating to human resources, financial management, information technology and estates. By one organisation taking on this responsibility for others or by jointly outsourcing to an external party it is hoped that there will be efficiencies of scale, improved quality through focused expertise and/or removal of functional barriers to closer working.

These concepts help to provide a prompt about what types of integration could be considered. Recognising the range of options helps to guide those responsible for leading a development as to where to focus their energies. It may also highlight an aspect that they had not yet considered but which could be vital. For example, in recognition of the increasing numbers of people with multiple long-term conditions there is a move for nurses working in general practice to undertake holistic reviews of people's health. This contrasts with previous guidance that emphasised that nurses should focus on a single condition at a time. This meant that patients with more than one condition would have to engage with multiple reviews which would often give similar advice regarding lifestyle changes. Often programmes seeking to introduce single reviews will focus on ensuring that nurses have sufficient time with people, that they have protocols to guide their interactions, and that people with more than one condition can be identified from the practice register. All of these aspects are important, but the approach also requires that nurses have sufficient knowledge of the different conditions and the skills to engage people in discussion about their overall health and wellbeing. This is often assumed but there is considerable evidence that this is not always the case.

The Rainbow Model

Many of the concepts outlined above are synthesised into a single taxonomy called the 'Rainbow' Model (Valentijn 2016). This was developed through a review of the academic literature and structured discussions with practice, policy and academic experts in the Netherlands. It proposes that the purpose of integration is to achieve the Triple Aims of better experiences of care, improved population health and more effective costs and utilisation. These purposes will be achieved through interactions between the four levels (or in the terms of the model 'dimensions') of a system. These relate to micro-integration (clinical), meso-levels (organisational and professional) and macro-level (system).

Clinical: The coordination of person-focused care in a single process across time, place and discipline. This relates to the 'integration of practice' in the toolkit.

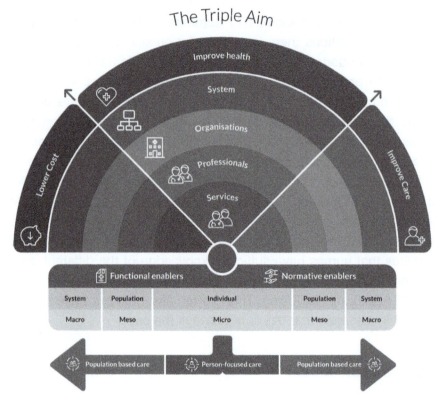

Figure 3.4 The Rainbow Model of Integrated Care

Professional: Inter-professional partnerships based on shared competences, roles, responsibilities and accountability. This relates
to the 'integration of learning' and 'services' in the toolkit.

Organisational: Inter-organisational relationships including common
governance mechanisms. This relates to the 'integration of
structures' in the toolkit.

System: A horizontally and vertically integrated system based on
a coherent set of (informal and formal) rules and policies
between providers and external stakeholders. This relates to
the 'integration of system governance' in the toolkit.

The model emphasises that there must be connection
between these dimensions. Progress in one level is unlikely to

be have much impact or be sustainable if there remain substantial barriers in other dimensions. This can be helped through developing a common way of understanding the problems and a shared commitment to how these will be addressed ('integration of values and vision'). Functional integration (i.e. 'integration of support functions' in the toolkit) can help to ensure that there are easy flows of information, funding and management data across the dimensions and agencies involved.

Reflect on a service which is familiar to you. This could be social work related or involve multiple professions. Using the Rainbow Model, try to map out the main agencies and other stakeholders who would need to collaborate to achieve the four dimensions of clinical, professional, organisational and system integration. If there are gaps in your knowledge about the agencies and stakeholders, undertake research to address these unknowns.

Theories of integration

Theories of systems

A fundamental principle of social work is that to support an individual we must understand the systems in which they live. This includes those systems that are more personal to the individual such as their family, friends and communities of choice or geography, and those related to wider society such as criminal justice, employment and welfare benefits. One of the major contributions that social workers bring to integrated care settings is to share such systems analysis with other professionals. This includes the many challenges that people face due to the inherent inequalities that can be promulgated by systems being designed for the many and not responsive or sympathetic to those with different situations and beliefs.

It can be argued that much of the thinking that has been used to construct and oversee our welfare services has not embraced theories of systems. Building on a tradition of 'scientific' approaches to management, improvements in care have been sought through breaking down service responses into a series of discrete but connected activities. The contribution of each activity is then considered and potential waste (i.e. unnecessary or harmful actions) identified in order to either remove it from the process or ensure that it is delivered more efficiently. Such linear approaches were developed in sectors such as manufacturing and logistics in which there is a predictable set of activities. LEAN is an example of such a methodology (Miller & Freeman 2015). This arose from the Japanese automobile industry in which there was an emphasis on 'continuous flow' across an entire process ('just-in-time') and 'intelligent systematisation' in which standardisation is used when helpful but not just to control employees ('jidoka'). LEAN has five main stages – specifying value from a customer perspective, identifying value stream, standardise to best practice, introduce 'pull' to overcome transitions and manage towards perfection. Such methodologies have been used successfully within some aspects of health and social care such as improving referral processes or operating theatre waiting times. However, they generally become unstuck when the phenomenon in question becomes too messy or great in scale as it then becomes impossible to break down the components into manageable pieces. This has been labelled as the danger of an 'atomistic' approach which then generates a particular set of responses from government to control through prescribed rules, rewards and punishments (Munro 2010).

Systems thinking recognises that there are many actors and activities involved in generating and maintaining a particular challenge faced by an individual or population. Its emphasis is on understanding how these relate and connect rather than focusing on the individual in depth. This was summed up by the creator of general systems theory in the 1960s as 'the whole is more than the sum of the parts' (Von Bertalanffy 1968, p55). There are numerous traditions within systems thinking such as open systems, cybernetics, system dynamics and soft systems. They all share though a common set of principles (Mingers & White 2010):

- Viewing the situation holistically, as opposed to reductionistically, as a set of diverse interacting elements within an environment.
- Recognising that the relationships or interactions between elements are more important than the elements themselves in determining the behaviour of the system.
- Recognising a hierarchy of levels of systems and the consequent ideas of properties emerging at different levels, and mutual causality both within and between levels.
- Accepting, especially in social systems, that people will act in accordance with differing purposes or rationalities.

Complex adaptive systems is a particular branch of thinking which has been applied to phenomenon as diverse as predicting the weather, investing in the stock markets and understanding of termite colonies. Such systems have been defined as 'a collection of individual agents with freedom to act in ways that are not always predictable, and whose actions are interconnected so that one agent's actions changes the context for other agents' (Plsek & Greenhalgh 2001). The system does not always have well defined boundaries with instead 'fuzziness' about who is a member of what system and fluctuation over time. The individual agents will respond to what they encounter through a set of internal rules – these may or may not be obvious to others. As the membership and the internal rules of agents can change, so the system can adapt over time. In doing so one complex adaptive system will interact and influence other systems with which it is connected. Despite the emergent and non-linear behaviour it is possible to detect overall patterns, and to identify 'attractors' which can influence agents to behave in particular ways (see Box 3.1).

Box 3.1 Complex adaptive systems within an integrated service

Within one rural area there were increasing demands on community health and social care services related to an ageing population. It was recognised that the professionals involved were not always working well together as they did not understand each other's roles and were most concerned with ensuring that their service was delivered to a good standard. The organisations responded through creating a joint service in which the nurses, social workers and therapists would be managed by a single lead. A shared referral process was created with a weekly multi-disciplinary meeting. The professionals were allocated to geographical localities and encouraged to see these as their core teams. Initially the service appeared to be running well with stronger relationships developed between the different professionals. New referrals were being seen in reasonable timescales with no major delays. Over time though the demands on the service continued to increase. It was noticed that it became harder to allocate new referrals with tensions between professional groups as to who should take lead responsibility. An evaluation discovered that staff continued to see their main allegiance to their professional peers rather than the integrated service. They generally had little sense of what the new service brought to their work or how it would improve care. They were willing to be flexible and collegiate only if their profession was seen to be working well, and if not then they would withdraw their support. The managers of the service reflected that they had not understood these internal rules or provided a strong enough rationale and vision to attract professionals to behave differently.

Complex adaptive thinking presents a very different scenario to be managed than that of a predictable and controllable set of ordered activities envisaged through scientific approaches. It suggests that what is important is looking at the 'big picture' and setting out an overall direction of travel for the system. Providing the minimum, rather than maximum, specifications which provide principles, resources and permissions gave the system and its actors the flexibility to respond creatively (Plsek & Wilson 2001). These should reflect the intrinsic motivators that bring most professionals into this work, such as improving people's lives and being able to practice at a high level. Double loop learning, in which organisations and partnerships seek not only to understand if they have successfully implemented a new policy but if the policy is actually of benefit, helps to provide challenge to compliant behaviour (Munro 2010). There needs to be a focus on developing the ability and capacity of a system to respond to future changes and opportunities and not just function in its current environment (Braithwaite et al. 2017). Often described as 'resilience', this can be fostered through a greater awareness of what enables us to provide good care and then using this as a basis for future development. This contrasts with our common emphasis on investigating only what has not gone well to avoid repeating the same mistakes.

Theories of boundaries

Open systems theory is concerned with understanding how organisations engage with their external environment (Morgan 2007). It suggests that entities have to develop sufficient diversity and capacity within their internal functions to cope with their environment – the 'requisite variety' – and that to survive in the long term this includes being able to evolve to cope with future changes. For social work organisations, this environment will include other social care organisations, regulatory frameworks, policy priorities and funding streams as well as more general issues such as the overall economy and availability of workforces. Within open systems it is expected that such entities will have a 'boundary' which provides a degree of separation between it and its environment. It will have some degree of control over this boundary so that it can influence what enters or leaves. This enables the entity to develop a steady state – 'homeostasis' – in which it can detect and respond to a deficit or surplus of resources or other factors. So, for example, a domiciliary care agency will have a referral process which it can 'open' or 'close' dependent on its capacity to support additional people and can only respond to an opportunity to work with a new population if it has staff with the necessary skills and the appropriate technology.

There are many boundaries to be considered in the field of social work and related sectors. These could for example be:

- physical (such as the fences around a particular location in which a service is provided or the geographical locality for which a local authority is responsible),
- resource based (such as the budget held by an organisation or the staff who they formally employ),
- legal (their statutory responsibilities for assessing need and arranging services and the limitations of their role),
- professional (what their staff are licensed to deliver and what their professional bodies will consider is appropriate),
- formality of care (there are often different expectations of what is reasonable to ask of family carers and the support that should be provided by them rather than by paid carers).

An obvious example of issues regarding the negotiation of a boundary relates to people who are ready to be discharged from hospital. Not only do they have to cross the physical boundary that separates their place of treatment from their home, but also the boundaries between acute and community-based health and social care organisations, rules about what is provided by the state and what is the responsibility of the individual and their family and so on. It is worth remembering that such boundaries occur within organisations as well as between those from different sectors. For example, there are often problems when people's need or situation dictates that they need to move between social work services for children and adults, or between specialist and generalist teams.

'Boundary spanning' is the process of trying to navigate such boundaries. One way is to designate specific individuals as 'boundary spanners' – 'individuals who have a dedicated job role or responsibility to work in a multi-agency and multi-sectoral environment and to engage in boundary-spanning activities, processes and practices' (Williams 2011, p27). Such roles are seen as involving four discrete but connected components – networker, entrepreneur, interpreter and organiser (Williams 2002):

Networker: Boundary spanners must have the ability to develop connections with the relevant actors and agencies in order to secure their support and influence their thinking. This requires relationship building and negotiating skills and can lead to them having considerable power through their social capital.

Entrepreneur: Whilst it is most often thought of in connection with private business, a similar process of recognising an opportunity that others have not made use of, mobilising resources in order to respond to this opportunity and generating new value as a consequence also applies within a public sector setting. This requires boundary spanners to be creative, flexible, visionary and persuasive.

Interpreter: More collaborative working involves the engagement of stakeholders who may have alternative world perspectives, professional traditions and views of what is most important to achieve. Enabling them to understand each other enough to have meaningful dialogue is an important facilitation role for a boundary spanner. This can lead to the subsequent development of trust between the partners.

Organiser: The range of networks, interests and opportunities open to a boundary spanner requires considerable discipline to plan and coordinate if these are going to be translated into sustainable value. This includes ordering and sharing the knowledge that they have gained from their diverse sources.

It is clear then that to work well those undertaking boundary spanning will need sufficient capacity, organisational support and freedom to pursue relationships and opportunities of potential value. It is also recognised as being a demanding undertaking due to for example the need to be able to operate in different institutional settings, to influence without power and to be able to cope with unclear governance and expectations (Williams 2012).

Theories of professions

Social work is one of many occupational groups that have reached the status of being described as a 'profession'. Whilst the concepts of 'professions' and 'professionals' are ones with which most people will be familiar there are alternative perspectives about what they mean and what, if any, benefits that they provide to society (Evetts 2003). An positive early view (e.g. Parsons 1951) was that professions enabled the development of a common set of competencies through defined educational routes, continuing training and socialisation into shared values relating to public benefits. Professional groups were seen to provide collegiate support to each other and to be worthy of trust from their clients, their employers and the general public. This combination of expertise and trustworthiness meant that they should be able to exercise discretion in their work with a minimum of outside interference. A more cynical perspective was that professions were motivated by self-interest which led them to protect their status, power, privilege and salaries through excluding others who could have potentially provided a similar function to society. Doctors are one of the most dominant in this regard through developing social contracts with the state with boundaries between the role of medical and other professions.

In recent times there has been a lessening of the trust that is placed in professionals. This is related to numerous scandals in which the behaviour of professionals has been shown to be less than exemplary (Crinson 2018). For example, the inquiry into high death rates of children following heart surgery in Bristol noted that senior doctors were able to practice in isolation and beyond the scrutiny of other team members. A professional culture that prized loyalty to colleagues above all else was reported as a contributory factor to the ability of Harold Shipman to continue working as a general practitioner. These and other inquiries resulted in changes in the way in which health professional bodies are licensed and regulated. For example, lay people became members of the General Medical Council and doctors were required to undergo revalidation every five years. Alongside these issues related specifically to professionals, there has also been a general trend towards a more managerialistic approach to the delivery of public services. This is connected with organisations playing a more active role in defining what is seen as being required of professions through setting out quality standards, role specifications and performance review processes (Evetts 2003). Sometimes called 'new professionalism', this is seen to be potentially diminishing the autonomy and discretion of professions. It is also resulting in the introduction of new roles such as physician assistants and nurse prescribers which are able to undertake tasks traditionally undertaken by a single profession.

Despite these threats to the existing professions, there is no doubt that some of them continue to hold considerable influence and that those responsible for improving services can find it difficult to encourage or require them to engage positively. One approach to addressing such barriers has been the development of 'hybrid' roles in which individuals continue with their professional work but also take on strategic management responsibilities.

Theories of governance

Governance is concerned with how the body accountable for a particular set of resources, activities and/or actors ensures that they complete their responsibilities to the required standard to achieve their overall purpose. It is relevant within multi-national corporations in relation to their profit-making enterprises (corporate governance), elected governments overseeing the delivery of services on behalf of their citizens (public governance) or trustees responsible for the work of a voluntary organisation (charitable governance). Examples of governance in social care relates to the professional regulation of those who are practicing as professional social workers, the licensing and inspection of providers delivering particular services such as foster care or residential care, and the purchasing of support from providers by commissioners. The World Health Organisation (2018) views governance as an essential element of a well-functioning health system and describes it as a 'political process that involves balancing competing influences and demands'. On a system level, governance has been described as the 'glue' that holds the other elements together (Mays 2018).

There have traditionally been three ideal forms of governance identified: market, hierarchy and network (Lowndes & Skelcher 1998):

1. Market relates to the exchange of property rights. Contracts set out the *price* and other conditions relating to these exchanges with disputes being settled through negotiation or through the courts. Markets are generally seen to involve low commitment between actors to enable flexibility to pursue their self-interests.
2. Hierarchy involves a central *authority* imposing a bureaucratic structure which specifies the responsibilities and expected behaviours of employed actors. Hierarchies control through salaries and the promise of future career opportunities. Those who fail to comply with the required routines and rituals risk the withdrawal of these benefits.
3. Network is based on a *reciprocal* arrangement in which the actors recognise a shared interest. This results in them making a longer-term commitment to working collaboratively.

Disagreements are addressed through dialogue and a wish to remain a member of the network.

Each idealised form is seen to have benefits. Markets enable actors to respond innovatively to opportunities and threats including the development of alliances with other actors if this would be advantageous. For public bodies, contracts provide a legal framework through which they can direct the activities of other parties and competition can be used to generate new ways of working and improved efficiencies. Hierarchies avoid the transactional costs of tenders and contracts with greater possibility of coordination due to the power of the central body. However, the emphasis on rules and internal regulations can lead to a loss of diversity of thinking as employees do not want to be seen as challenging the established order. Networks' shared commitment to a common interest and mutual respect between members should encourage more openness to new ideas and exchange of learning. That said, it has also been highlighted that they may be most interested in benefits for their members at a cost to those outside of the network. It is clear that no governance approach is better per se, with much depending on the context and purpose intended. It is therefore common for multiple forms of governance to be applied simultaneously within the same area of public service. This can also reflect difference between what has historically been the norm within that area (and which may be hard to unpick due to the power of incumbents) and new governance arrangements for programmes that have been introduced more recently.

Integration can involve bringing together entities that are subject to different governance processes both internally as organisations and from their external environment. Unless there is explicit sharing of their governance responsibilities then the partners involved may not even fully understand how their requirements may differ. Similarly, the professionals they are involved with have their own regulatory requirements that will include a defined 'scope of practice'. Those leading integrated care programmes need to assess what if any additional governance arrangements are required and how these could encourage the necessary changes in behaviours. Partnerships between organisations have been described as experiencing a 'life cycle', with alternative forms of governance likely at different stages of this lifecycle (Lowndes & Skelcher 1998) (see Box 3.2).

Box 3.2 Life stages of partnerships (Lowndes & Skelcher 1998)

Pre-partnership collaboration is characterised by a network mode of governance based upon informality, trust and a sense of common purpose.

Partnership creation and consolidation is characterised by hierarchy based upon an assertion of status and authority differentials and the formalisation of procedures.

Partnership programme delivery is characterised by market (or quasi-market) mechanisms of tendering and contract, with low levels of co-operation between providers.

Partnership termination or succession is characterised by a re-assertion of a network governance mode as a means to maintain agency commitment, community involvement and staff employment.

Models of integration

House of care

The House of Care was originally developed by the Year of Care Partnerships. This is an NHS organisation based in Northumberland, England. Its purpose is to improve how professionals engage with people and their families so that the focus is about what matters to them and they are actively engaged in decisions and actions to promote their own wellbeing. Following work with many different organisations and localities the Year of Care Partnerships developed the House of Care model (Coulter et al. 2013). This represents the components that need to be in place and provides a helpful metaphor to engage with local stakeholders. Following successful pilots in Lothian, Glasgow and Tayside, the House of Care model has been adopted across Scotland.

At the heart of the House of Care is the support planning process. This is seen as a shared conversation between two sources of expertise: the person, who has lived experience of their own life, and the professional, who has technical expertise based on their training and skills. To be meaningful, this will require effective communication between these two experts, that is based on eliciting the capacities, needs and preferences of the person. The

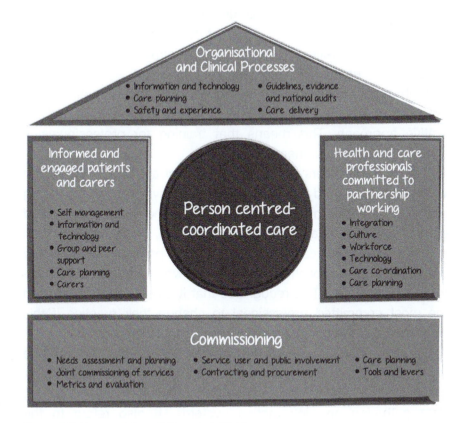

Figure 3.5 House of Care (Miller et al. 2016)

documentary care plan that emerges is a representation of this process rather than the main outcome to be achieved. The walls of the House of Care are necessary for these new conversations to be undertaken.

The left wall: engaged and informed people. People need to be prepared for this different type of conversation with a health or care professional. This means that they need to understand what the process will entail, feel confident in speaking differently to the professional, have sufficient knowledge of health systems and how they operate, and feel 'activated' to contribute to discussions and activities related to their health.

The right wall: professionals committed to partnerships. There are two main partnerships for professionals within the house – with the people concerned and with other professionals. In relation to people, the professional must recognise that they may not previously have practiced in a patient centric manner. This can be challenging, but reflects what people commonly report through experience surveys. It can require the practical, i.e., having enough time to spend with someone, and the attitudinal, i.e., believing that people are capable of responding to a more collaborative approach. This means that training for professionals is a central part of implementation.

The roof: this refers to the organisational and policy context in which the care and support planning conversations are being undertaken. It can include factors such as the range and style of general information and care documentation, the extent to which information systems can record and prompt professionals to follow a more holistic approach, and the way in which the available workforce are deployed. This recognises that it can be difficult for even the most committed professional to change their practice if this contrasts with the processes and rules to which they work.

The foundation: these are the resources that must be in place for the house to be able to operate. It includes those needed for the individual conversations such as consultation time, training, data gathering and information systems. It also refers to the assets within the local community that can support people to maintain their health and wellbeing. This will entail mapping out what is available and working with community groups to address common gaps in what is available.

Developmental Model of Integrated Care

The Developmental Model of Integrated Care (Figure 3.6) attempts to set out the main elements that need to be considered when creating a new programme for integrated care (Minkman 2016). It is not specific to a particular population or issue as it does not recommend particular interventions as such. The focus is instead on the process of development. It is based on a literature review of the main elements of integrated care, a three round discursive process with 31 experts and then a concept mapping of the 89 elements selected by the experts. It was then validated by being tested out by integrated care coordinators of services in the Netherlands. A self-assessment tool has been produced that enables those leading projects to gain the views of partners of the stages of development and what should be strengthened.

The model is based around nine clusters of integrated care which then contain a number of elements that are necessary to implement the cluster.

Cluster 1: Patient-centredness: Information flows tailored to specific (sub)groups of patients. Elements focus on integrated patient and care process supporting information such as front offices, self-management support or information systems and delivering care adjusted to individual needs.

Cluster 2. Delivery system: Coordination mechanism sand procedures for streamlining the care process for the whole care chain is the main focus of this cluster. This includes reaching all agreements (e.g. logistics, sharing expertise), procedures (e.g. information exchange) or tools (e.g. care plans) in the care chain.

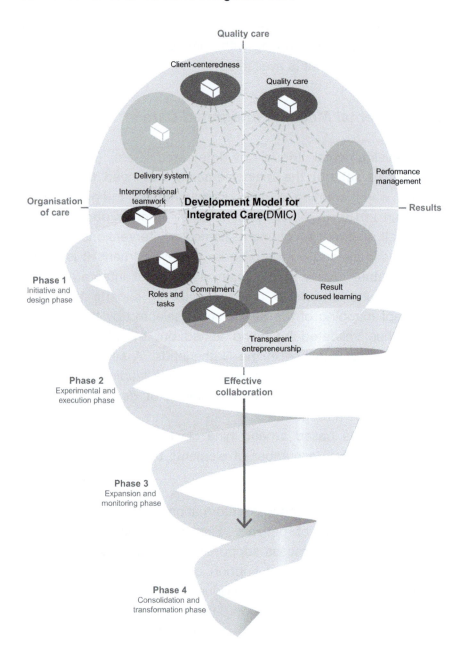

Figure 3.6 Developmental Model of Integrated Care (Minkman 2016)

Cluster 3. Performance management: Measurement and analyses of the results of the care delivered in the care chain. Elements address performance targets at all levels, indicators related to client outcomes, client judgements, organisational outcomes and financial performance data.

Cluster 4. Quality care: The design of a multidisciplinary care pathway throughout the care chain, based on evidence-based guidelines and clients' needs and preferences. A needs assessment of the specific client group is required for this purpose, combined with the involvement of client representatives in designing, improving and monitoring the integrated care.

Cluster 5. Result-focused learning: A learning climate of striving towards continuously improved results in the care chain is this cluster's central theme. The elements address essential ingredients for improvement: defining goals for collaboration, identifying bottlenecks and gaps in care, and ways of learning and exchanging knowledge in an open atmosphere.

Cluster 6. Inter-professional teamwork: The defined client group is the population to be reached by collaborating professionals, working in well-organised multidisciplinary teams in the care chain.

Cluster 7. Roles and tasks: The need for clarity about each other's expertise, roles and tasks in the care chain. Effective collaboration at all levels, of which new partners and allocating coordinating roles are the main components.

Cluster 8. Commitment: The commitment of leaders of the care chain to clearly defined goals and a collaborative ambition.

Cluster 9. Transparent entrepreneurship: Space for innovation (experiments), leadership responsibilities for performance achievement and joint financial agreements covering the integrated care.

The Developmental Model recognises that there will be phases of implementation. This begins with a *design* phase in which the partners recognise there is an opportunity and agree to working together to better service an identified group. The *execution* phase involves piloting new ways of working and the forming of roles, protocols and formal agreements. The *expansion* stage is when the learning from projects becomes systematised and implemented in other areas. Data on process and outcomes is analysed to identify further improvements. The final stage is the *transformation* stage in which the host organisations recognise how they need to adapt their overall structures to facilitate more general implementation of integrated care. The self-assessment asks respondents to identify which elements are being planned and which have been implemented with the assumption that as the programme moves through the phases there will be an increasing number that have been implemented.

The World Health Organisation framework

The World Health Organisation adopted a framework for integrated care in 2016 (WHO 2016). This was based on a wide-ranging consultation with experts at the national, regional and global level and on the experience of coordinating care in different countries. Its purpose is to outline the strategies that countries need to adopt if they are to ensure that their systems are equitable, safe and sustainable. Due to the many differences between low, middle and high income countries the World Health Organisation has not suggested a single template but rather a framework that can be adapted to local circumstances.

Strategy 1: Empowering and engaging people and communities
Empowering and engaging people is about providing the opportunity, skills and resources that people need to be articulate and empowered users of health services and advocates for a reformed health system. This strategy seeks to unlock community and individual resources for action at all levels.
Strategy 2: Strengthening governance and accountability
Strengthening governance requires a participatory approach to policy formulation, decision-making and performance evaluation at all levels of the health system, from policy-making to

the clinical intervention level. Establishing a strong policy framework and a compelling narrative for reform will be important to building a shared vision, as well as setting out how that vision will be achieved.

Strategy 3: Reorientating the model of care

Reorienting the model of care means ensuring that efficient and effective health care services are designed, purchased and provided through innovative models of care that prioritise primary and community care services and the co-production of health. It requires investment in holistic and comprehensive care, including health promotion and ill-health prevention strategies that support people's health and wellbeing.

Strategy 4: Coordinating services within and across sectors

Services should be coordinated around the needs and demands of people. This requires integration of providers within and across health care settings, development of referral systems and networks among levels of care, and the creation of linkages between health and other sectors. It encompasses intersectoral action at the community level in order to address the social determinants of health and optimise use of scarce resources.

Strategy 5: Creating an enabling environment

For the four previous strategies to become an operational reality, it is necessary to create an enabling environment that brings together all stakeholders to undertake transformational change. This complex task will involve a diverse set of processes to bring about the necessary changes in leadership and management, reorientation of the workforce, legislative frameworks and incentives.

An on-line learning network has been created by the World Health Organisation to enable professionals, organisations and policy makers to share learning about how to implement the strategies (www.integratedcare4people.org/practices/). This contains a wide range of resources and good practice examples. Alongside the network, there is formal support available from the World

Health Organisation to countries seeking to progress the strategies. This includes developing the capacity of health leaders, providing technical assistance and consolidating local evidence to build a case for change.

During the social work qualification you will learn about a range of social science theories. Do any of these have potential relevance to integrated care? If so, what insights could they bring and how does this suggest that social work practice could be improved?

Further resources

Health and Social Care in the Community https://onlinelibrary.wiley.com/journal/13,652,524

Health and Social Care in the Community is an international peer-reviewed journal with a multidisciplinary audience. The journal promotes critical thinking and informed debate about all aspects of health and social care. Original papers are sought that reflect the broad range of policy, practice and theoretical issues underpinning the provision of care in the community.

Institute for Healthcare Improvement www.ihi.org

The Institute for Healthcare Improvement (IHI) is an independent not-for-profit organisation based in the US. For more than 25 years it has been a leading innovator, convener, partner and driver of results in health and care improvement worldwide.

IntegratedCare4People www.integratedcare4people.org

IntegratedCare4People is an online network of practitioners and organisations from around the world working together to encourage health systems and services to be integrated and people-centred.

It has been developed by the World Health Organisation to support the implementation of the global framework.

International Journal of Integrated Care www.ijic.org

The *International Journal of Integrated Care* (IJIC) is an online, open-access, peer-reviewed scientific journal that publishes original articles in the field of integrated care on a continuous basis.

References

Braithwaite, J., Churruca, K., Ellis, L. A., C Long, J., Clay-Williams, R., Damen, N. ... Ludlow, K. (2017). *Complexity science in healthcare-aspirations, approaches, applications and accomplishments: a white paper*. Sydney: Macquarie University.

Coulter, A., Roberts, S., & Dixon, A. (2013). *Delivering better services for people with long-term conditions: building the House of Care*. London: King's Fund.

Crinson, I. (2018). The health professions and professional practice. In Scrambler, G. (ed.). (2018). *Sociology as applied to medicine e-book*. London: Palgrave, 319–337.

Evetts, J. (2003). The sociological analysis of professionalism: occupational change in the modern world. *International Sociology*, *18*(2), 395–415.

Glouberman, S., & Zimmerman, B. (2002). Complicated and complex systems: what would successful reform of Medicare look like? *Romanow Papers*, *2*, 21–53.

Health & Social Care Alliance. (2018). *The House of Care Model*. Available at: www.alliance-scotland.org.uk/health-and-social-care-support-and-services/house-of-care/house-of-care-model/ (downloaded 05.11.2018)

Lowndes, V., & Skelcher, C. (1998). The dynamics of multi-organizational partnerships: an analysis of changing modes of governance. *Public Administration*, *76*(2), 313–333.

Mays, N. (2018). Health care systems. In Scambler, G. (ed.). (2008). *Sociology as applied to medicine e-book*. London: Palgrave.

Miller, R., Brown, H., & Mangan, C. (2016). *Integrated care in action: a practical guide for health, social care and housing support*. London: Jessica Kingsley.

Miller, R., & Freeman, T. (2015). *Managing change in social care*. London: SSCR.

Mingers, J., & White, L. (2010). A review of the recent contribution of systems thinking to operational research and management science. *European Journal of Operational Research, 207*(3), 1147–1161.

Minkman, M. (2016). The Development Model for Integrated Care: a validated tool for evaluation and development. *Journal of Integrated Care, 24*(1), 38–52.

Morgan, G. (2007). *Images of organization*. Thousand Oaks

Munro, E. (2010). *The Munro review of child protection interim report: the child's journey*. Available at: https://assets.publishing.service.gov.uk/government/uploads/system/uploads/attachment_data/file/624946/DFE-00010-2011.pdf (downloaded 05.11.2018)

Parsons, T. (1951). *The social system*. London: Tavistock.

Plsek, P. E., & Greenhalgh, T. (2001). Complexity science: the challenge of complexity in health care. *BMJ: British Medical Journal, 323*(7313), 625.

Plsek, P. E., & Wilson, T. (2001). Complexity science: complexity, leadership, and management in healthcare organisations. *BMJ: British Medical Journal, 323*(7315), 746.

Valentijn, P. P. (2016). Rainbow of Chaos: a study into the theory and practice of integrated primary care. *International Journal of Integrated Care, 16*(2), 3.

Von Bertalanffy, L. (1968). *General systems theory* (Rev. ed.). New York: Braziller.

Williams, P. (2002). The competent boundary spanner. *Public Administration, 80*(1), 103–124.

Williams, P. (2011). The life and times of the boundary spanner. *Journal of Integrated Care, 19*(3), 26–33.

Williams, P. (2012). *Collaboration in public policy and practice: perspectives on boundary spanners*. Bristol: Policy Press.

World Health Organisation. (2016). *Framework on integrated, people-centred health services*. Available at: www.who.int/servicedelivery safety/areas/people-centred-care/en/ (downloaded 05.11.2018)

World Health Organisation. (2018). *Governance in health systems*. Available at: www.who.int/healthsystems/topics/stewardship/en/ (downloaded 05.11.2018).

4 Evidence of integrated care

Evidence is an important means to evaluate if the thinking that lies behind new policies and programmes has resulted in the expected benefits. A good theory should be supported by research which demonstrates that its principles translate as expected in the real world. Integrated care should therefore be as informed as other areas of practice by robust studies of its implementation and impact. Equally it must be remembered that there are debates regarding the concept of evidence-based practice and what should be seen as evidence. Health care fields tend to have a more traditional view of what constitutes evidence that are based on positivist knowledge paradigms. These see research within a strict hierarchy with randomised control trials as producing the most reliable evidence. Social work will approach evidence from a more constructivist perspective with values from diverse sources including the views of people, families and communities. This has led to the concept of 'evidence informed' rather than 'evidence based' practice (McLaughlan & Teater 2017). This applies to those deciding on policy directions as well as frontline professionals. Commissioners, for example, are partly informed by formal research evidence but this is considered alongside their previous experience and insights provided by colleagues doing similar roles (Miller et al. 2014).

Alongside these debates about the nature and importance of evidence are critiques of what has been studied and what has been neglected by research. Areas such as education and health have tended to receive more funding from research bodies in comparison to that invested in social work and supported housing. This means that systematic reviews are more likely to support a health-based intervention than a social work one due to the weight of evidence that is available. The World Health Organisation highlighted this issue when it undertook an evidence review to support the development of its framework for integrated care.

> Research studies have typically focused on treatment and diagnosis, and adult and elderly care, meaning that the evidence base for other services is less strong, as is evidence on other life stages (such as childhood)
>
> ... Overall, it is striking how the bulk of evidence, and particularly higher quality studies, focus on relatively narrowly-defined interventions to support people-centred and integrated health services.
>
> (WHO 2015, p6)

Despite these gaps the World Health Organisation assessed there was sufficient evidence to be confident that integration is an essential component of a high performing health and care system. This section will present the evidence for the impact of integrated care and what can support its implementation. It begins with reflecting on the evidence that fragmented care can lead to children and adults being placed at risk.

Social work is based on a constructivist paradigm which recognises there is more than one way to see an issue with no single 'truth' in many situations. Can you think of a circumstance in which you saw an issue very differently to another professional? How do you think they will have come to an alternative conclusion from you and what merit did their position hold?

Fragmentation and safeguarding

If abuse or neglect results in the death or serious harm of a child, then all of the home nations require that a multi-agency review is undertaken. These reviews have been referred to differently across the UK – Child Safeguarding Practice Reviews in England, Case

Management Reviews in Northern Ireland, Significant Case Reviews in Scotland, Child Practice Reviews in Wales – but all have a common purpose to identify learning which can help protect children and young people in the future (NSPCC 2018). Similar arrangements are in place regarding local partners reviewing their individual and collective response to complex or serious cases involving adults. These reports provide detailed insights into what can be improved in relation to the safeguarding of vulnerable children and adults. In this section we will consider those relevant to integration in relation to different populations and localities.

Thematic analysis of child reviews across the UK

The National Society for the Protection of Cruelty to Children (NSPCC) co-ordinates a UK repository in collaboration with the Association of Independent Local Safeguarding Children's Boards. At September 2018 this held over 800 case reviews and inquiry reports dating back to 1945. The NSPCC uses these reviews to provide thematic analysis which focus on specific types of abuse and/or specific groups of children and young people. Case reviews relating to children and young people who are deaf and/or disabled published since 2010 (NSPCC 2016) report that families can be overwhelmed by the number and diversity of professionals and services who are providing support and unsure about which professional is best to approach about an issue. Professionals received different information about the child and their family and if no consistent approach were in place then this (and linked concerns) were not shared. As a result, no agency could gain a complete picture of the situation and risk. It was often health professionals who held the most information, but they saw issues relating to safeguarding as being the responsibility of social services and outside their professional remit. A similar failure to share important information features in reviews of young people displaying harmful sexual behaviour. This was not helped by such young people often not being discussed at multi-agency meetings (NSPCC 2017). Alternative use of terminology again led to communication deficits in relation to families in which there was domestic violence (NSPCC 2013). Generic and less serious terms such as 'arguing with partner' or 'family problems' resulted in other agencies not recognising the level of risk that a child or young person was facing. A diminution of risk also occurred when a perpetrator was not charged even if there was still significant danger to the child (and indeed the partner). This was due to other agencies not fully understanding the decision-making processes within the criminal justice system.

Safeguarding adult reviews in London

This report undertook an analysis of 27 Safeguarding Adult Reviews (SAR) completed by London safeguarding adults boards between 1 April 2015 and 30 April 2017 (Braye & Preston-Shoot 2017). One of its principle themes referred to inter-professional and interagency collaboration. It concluded that 'agencies tended to work in parallel lines, lacking a joint or shared approach, or any sense of shared ownership' (p36). Service coordination was an issue in 23 out of the 27 reports. Care plans were not developed on a multi-agency basis or those developed by single organisations even shared with partner agencies. There was a lack of understanding about other professionals' roles and a common inertia caused by blaming of others for lack of action or decision making. This was more likely if there were no interagency meetings. This resulted in several examples of significant risks being poorly managed as there was no clarity about who was leading or a focus by the agencies on only one aspect of the person's life. In other examples meetings were held but not all of the agencies participated. There was a reluctance to follow up the outcomes of a referral when no response had been received to ensure that it had been properly considered. Despite formal processes being in place, there was a similar reticence to escalate concerns to more senior levels when no or insufficient action had been taken. Eleven out of the 27 SARs reported that there was insufficient 'safeguarding literacy' regarding how the system should operate and the individual responsibilities of professionals and how they could interact. 'Legal literacy' was highlighted in relation to mental capacity assessments, the possibility of criminal prosecution and transition from child to adult services. A lack of shared information and a failure to communicate effectively was raised in 23 out of the 27. Problems included a failure to recognise what information would be helpful to others, insufficient detail in the information transferred and delays in necessary information being provided. These were caused by a lack of comprehensive data sharing protocols or the lack of introduction of a shared recording system. In some cases these systems were technically in place but there was not a comprehensive implementation process which included training and monitoring. Interagency issues were a problem in the review process due to a failure of relevant agencies being asked to participate or declining the invitation.

Significant case reviews in Scotland

The Care Inspectorate reviewed 20 Significant Case Reviews undertaken between 2012 and 2015 which involved 23 children and young people (Care Inspectorate 2016). Many reported that a lack of interagency communication and silo working by professionals and services had contributed to risks not being properly recognised or acted upon. Shared recording systems were rare which meant that it was down to an individual professional to realise the importance of information that they held and to effectively communicate to others. This made it more likely that there could be human errors in the processing of information which was exacerbated if the professional in question did not attend or failed to contribute this information at multi-agency decision-making meetings. In other cases, information was communicated to others, but they did not recognise its importance and therefore did not act appropriately on its implications. This was sometimes due to the information being of a specialist nature (e.g. legal or health) but with insufficient explanation to enable non-specialists to fully grasp its significance. Agencies failed to communicate to others when they were ending their involvement with a child or family. This included situations in which the family was not settled in one locality as there was confusion about which social care and health agencies had responsibility for the coordination and delivery of support. Some professionals saw their role as being solely to share concerns with the social worker who had been identified as the lead professional. As a consequence they did not contribute their perspective to multi-agency discussions or challenge conclusions with which they did not agree in meetings or through agreed escalation protocols. The Care Inspectorate described this as a lack of 'collective responsibility' to keep children safe.

Safeguarding adult reviews focusing on self-neglect

This research considered 134 Safeguarding Adult Reviews in England which related to self-neglect (Preston-Shoot 2018). Self-neglect includes refusal of services, lack of self-care and lack of care of one's environment. It found that there were four cross-cutting domains – practice with the individual adult, the professional team around the adult, organisations around the professional team and interagency governance. Therefore three domains (and arguably all four if integrated care is seen to be person centred), raise issues relevant to integration. There were concerns regarding the relationship of commissioners and providers and the exclusion of some providers from networks designed to promote more holistic care. Safeguarding Adult Reviews reported a poor awareness of joint procedures, and a failure to follow these in practice (in particular to organise multiagency meetings). The majority of concerns related to professional joint working between children's and adult social services, hospital and community-based health care services, police and mental health services. Agencies were described as preferring to refer people on rather than working with other services to develop an appropriate solution. This led to people being passed back and forth as agencies refused to accept responsibility. There was a lack of shared approach to assessment, case management and contingency planning which resulted in poor coordination and disjointed experience of services. Multi-agency meetings were often not held and when they were these were not always well structured. Furthermore, professional or agency hierarchies resulted in some perspectives not being heard or their concerns minimised. Combined with a lack of effective information sharing, this meant that people were not supported through times of transition in particular. This included discharge from hospital and transfer between teams when the individual had remained in the same environment.

Evidence of impact

Table 4.1 provides an overview of major evidence reviews which have sought to understand the impact of 'integration' for different populations and/or in respect of a particular service area. Despite being highly selective about the standards of evidence these reviews were able to identify many studies that they have been able to draw upon. All of the reviews which considered outcomes for people and their families expressed concerns at the strength of the evidence base and recommended more research be undertaken (Box 4.1).

The evidence that is available suggests there can be benefits in relation to people's experience of accessing care, and various elements of their quality of life. Baxter et al. (2018) also found that integrated care leads to increased patient access, including a reduction in waiting times, and suggest that overall integrated care leads to increased satisfaction from users and carers. Whilst Atkinson et al. (2007) found little empirical evidence for impact on service users they did report one frequent benefit as being improved access to services. Rummery (2009) identifies that there have been improvements for people with mental health problems in relation to better quality of life and transition from hospital to community. She also found that there was greater awareness by

---

Box 4.1 Outcomes for people and families

There seems to be very little empirical evidence for the impact on service users. The evidence available suggests that the main benefit to service users is likely to centre around improved access to services, but more research needs to be conducted in this area.

(Atkinson et al. 2007, pp4–5)

On the one hand the evidence for improved outcomes for users is there, although it is equivocable and at times difficult to link particular outcomes with … partnership work/joined up governance . On the other hand … there is limited (but not non-existent) evidence to suggest that partnership work between health and social care leads to user-defined priorities being taken seriously in the planning and delivery of welfare.

(Rummery 2009, p182)

We identified surprisingly little evidence regarding the impact of integrated care models on patient experiences of services, beyond measures of reported patient satisfaction. There seems a need for further attention to how reconfiguration impacts on patients and carers, including whether service users perceive any change, or have greater knowledge of or involvement in services.

(Baxter et al. 2018, p9)

---

professionals of the challenges facing family carers. This review highlights benefits for children and young people, in particular those with mental health problems and/or a learning disability, with improved satisfaction for parents and families even when the aims of services (typically to reduce costs) are not met. Finally, Rummery also notes that collaboration between disciplines and services has successfully provided and/or increased access to services for those who are often excluded from mainstream support. This includes those who are homeless, from minority ethnic communities and in rural settings. Looman and colleagues (2016) reports that integrated approaches seeking to prevent deterioration of older frail people[1] show promising outcomes in regard to overall wellbeing and satisfaction with life. People also felt empowered to participate in decisions over their care and in tasks of daily living.

Perhaps reflecting the emphasis in governmental policy, much more research activity has focused on the economic impacts of integration. Economic impacts have centred around three areas: *utilisation* (i.e., the level of use of a particular service over a designated time period); *cost-effectiveness* (i.e., the benefits of an intervention in respect of an identified unit of currency such as life years gained or quality adjusted life years (QALYs), or *cost and expenditure* (including costs that have been avoided through the integrated care intervention) (Nolte & Pitchforth 2014). Much of the research has focused on utilisation rates within hospital services. Damery et al. (2016) found that around half of the reviews that considered emergency admissions, readmissions and length of stay reported reductions, but the level of reduction in activity varied considerably between 15 per cent and 50 per cent. There was a more positive effect if the integrated care interventions were targeting a single health condition. Whilst there was variation between the conditions being studied, Martínez-González et al. (2014) also reported reductions in hospital activity. Both reviews though report that there was no consistent reduction in costs. There is also the potential that there is not a saving across the system as a whole, but rather a 'shunting' of activity from one service to another. Loomans and colleagues (2016) highlights that decreases in hospital activity are often associated with an increase in use of primary care services. This review also explored potential correlation cost (effectiveness), and the type and intensity of integration. For hospital length of stay, there was no organisational and financial integration in the interventions that generated a decrease in length of stay, whereas the interventions that had an increase in length of stay were integrated both

Table 4.1 Major evidence reviews of the impact of integration

Author	Date	Population	Focus	Methodology	Number of studies
Atkinson et al.	2007	Multi-agency working in children's services	Models, impacts, facilitators and challenges to multi-agency working	Literature review of evidence published between 2000 and 2007 and case studies	29 primary research studies
Rummery	2009	All populations, including people with mental health problems, children and those from 'hard to reach' communities	Patient/user outcomes associated with public partnerships (health and social care, private/voluntary sector, patients/users)	Purposive literature review of articles published between 1997 and 2007	76 articles
Nolte & Pitchforth	2014	Adults including those with mental health problems and older people	Economic impacts of integrated care approaches	Rapid review of systematic reviews published between 2004 and	19 articles
Baxter et al.	2018	All populations (but must include interaction with health care services)	Effects of models of integrated care on efficiency, effectiveness and quality of care	Systematic review of evidence published between 2006 and 2017	167 primary research studies
Martínez-González et al.	2014	Adults with chronic conditions	Patient-centred outcomes, process quality, use of health care resources and costs	Meta review of systematic reviews and meta-analyses published up to 2012	27 systematic reviews reporting on 824 primary research studies

(Continued)

Table 4.1 (Cont.)

Author	Date	Population	Focus	Methodology	Number of studies
Looman et al.	2018	Older people living in the community identified as being frail	Effectiveness and cost-effectiveness of preventative and integrative care	Systematic review of studies published up to 2016	46 primary research studies
Damery et al.	2016	Adult patients with one or more chronic disease	Effectiveness of integrated care interventions in reducing hospital activity	Umbrella review of systematic reviews published up to 2015	50 reviews of 1208 primary studies
Cameron et al.	2014	Adults living in the UK	Joint working between health and social care	Review of articles published between 2000 and 2011	30 primary research studies

organisationally and financially. Similarly, the one intervention that resulted in a decrease in primary care had no functional, organisational and financial integration, whereas this was both present and absent for interventions that found no effect or an increase in primary care utilisation. Damery et al. (2016) do not look at intensity as such but do recommend that multi-interventional programmes are more successful than those focused on a single approach.

Baxter et al. (2018) conclude that integration does not lead to 'unequivocally positive effects' and suggest that 'new models of care may be best targeted to particular patient groups (such as those with complex needs) rather than being seen as a panacea for all' (p9). Atkinson et al. (2007) agree, but raise that working more closely with professionals from other disciplines and services can be rewarding and stimulating for staff. They do provide a note of caution though regarding the potential for increased demands on professionals through being asked to undertake additional activities and to provide improved access to services.

Evidence of barriers

Alongside studies of the impact of integrated care are those which consider the implementation of programmes (Table 4.2). Such evidence is important as there are many examples of pilots that have initially demonstrated positive benefits but have failed to sustain these into the long term. There can also be challenges when what has worked well in one area is transferred to another. Such difficulties of implementation are of course not confined to integrated care. The requirement to achieve change across multiple services and sectors that have not previously collaborated does lead to particular complications. Furthermore approaches to innovation which have worked in a single sector may not translate in our settings. This is summarised by the Chief Executive of the International Foundation of Integrated Care as follows:

> we have come a long way in being able to articulate the key building blocks of integrated care, the interplay between them is so complex and intertwined that it seems an impossible challenge to create any simple implementation model. Yet, if integrated care is to advance, we must become better at smoothing over the many obstacles and challenges to implementation that have bedevilled the uptake and roll-out of even the most proven of integrated care interventions.
>
> (Goodwin 2016)

Professional barriers

Potential for conflict between professions is rife. By their nature, professionals have confidence in their particular knowledge and skill base which may lead to a different interpretation of a situation than that of other professionals. There is often an established hierarchy between professions which enables decisions to be made in the traditional silos. Integrated settings can lead to accepted compromises being challenged. If one profession is in a minority then this can amplify these challenges. For example, social workers have reported feeling undervalued in health dominated community mental health teams and at its most extreme, experience their core values as being under threat. Different attitudes towards risk assessment and what is an acceptable level of risk is a common source of tension between professions. This can lead to impasses regarding how best an individual's needs should be addresses and lead to care being stuck at a particular step of a pathway. All parties have to understand respective roles and responsibilities but often this is not the case, leading to a failure to introduce even basic processes such as joint assessment and care planning processes. Such clarity is also needed at a strategic level – partnership groups need a defined role and clear expectation of their members. Professionals can be reluctant to consider undertaking new tasks, whilst also resisting other professionals accepting responsibilities that would have traditionally fallen to their discipline. Too great flexibility can though lead to confusion and professional working outside of their scope of practice.

Not understanding the roles and skills of others can prevent professionals from making the most of new opportunities to collaborate. Linked to this, a lack of trust, i.e., to be confident that a colleague from a different professional group will behave responsibly and take appropriate action, may result in concerns about delegating tasks or sharing risks. Not being located together or at least not having regular opportunities for interaction, adds to professional distance and difficulties in seeing others as being trustworthy. Similarly, a failure to invest in shared development events can result in poorly formed teams. Professionals may lack skills in working more collaboratively as this may not have been fostered in their prior careers. Separate management structures and clashes in organisational cultures make it difficult for professionals from different backgrounds to feel comfortable and supported in their practice. For example, the level of autonomy afforded by management regarding their professional judgement and professionals' ability to allocate resources in response to an individual's need varied between health and care organisations. Different terms and conditions, and in particular financial rewards, can foster resentment between professional groups.

Organisational barriers

Competing visions by organisations of the purpose of the partnership and incompatible aspirations about the individual benefits that will be accrued present early barriers to the development of more integrated care. A failure to agree who will lead the collaboration will prevent coordination and affect decision making. This will also be affected by different governance processes and attitudes to risk. For example, partnerships can struggle to agree on acceptable working arrangements for staff and sufficient evidence to enable investment of new resources. A lack of history of success in collaboration across organisations (and the senior managers that lead them) results in a more tentative approach to new opportunities for integration. A difference of scale and influence can lead to power imbalances, particularly if one or more organisations is dependent on other partners for resources or legitimacy. A policy environment which does not encourage (or demand) more integrated working through the investment of resources, performance frameworks and regulatory processes will foster continued working within sectorial and professional boundaries. That said, a government mandate to integrate which does not give sufficient time for appropriate relationships and shared plans to be developed may add to organisational tensions. A market governance approach in which partners may be bidding for the same resources can make them less willing to share good practice as they may lose their competitive advantage. Tender processes that require partnerships to be developed can encourage new alliances being formed, although these may be dependent on the particular contract being maintained.

Table 4.2 Major evidence reviews of the implementation of integrated care

Author	Date	Population	Focus	Methodology	Number of studies
Atkinson et al.	2007	Multi-agency working in children's services	Models, impacts, facilitators and challenges to multi-agency working	Literature review of evidence published between 2000 and 2007 and case studies	29 primary research studies
Cameron et al.	2014	Adults living in the UK	Joint working between health and social care	Review of articles published between 2000 and 2011	30 primary research studies
Seaton et al.	2018	All populations	Organisational collaboration for health promotion	Scoping review of articles published between 2001 and 2015	25 articles
Hujala et al.	2016	Adults with multi-morbidities	Implementation of integration	Literature review and investigation of 101 innovative programmes across Europe	60 articles
Auschra	2018	All populations	Barriers to inter-organisation collaboration in health care	Systematic review of articles published up to 2017	40 articles

Normative barriers

A shared view of aims and objectives across organisations is central to success but it can be hard to communicate this sufficiently to foster engagement from operational management and frontline professionals. Not understanding or agreeing with the vision, can result in professionals and managers being unwilling to commit to the changes in roles, relationships and behaviours that more integrated care may demand. Engaging stakeholders, including staff and people who will access services, can help to develop a more

relevant vision and convince those involved that there is a genu-
ineness and transparency in the approach. A failure to engage
others in the development of a vision and plan leads to mistrust
and scepticism, with connected challenges for implementation of
the strategy. In many ways this can be summarised as a lack of
effective leadership.

Functional barriers

Legal difficulties with information sharing, both actual and perceived,
can result in delays in necessary exchanges of information and more
cumbersome processes than are required. Where information sharing
protocols can be agreed, there may still be incompatibility of electronic record systems which results in professionals not having timely
access to the necessary details. Alternative ethics processes and
interpretations of what is accepted ethically, can similarly challenge
research projects of integration across different sectors. A lack of
resources to support the transformation process can make it difficult
to generate sufficient momentum. Time limited project funds can help
but there are often then major problems when temporary funding
ends. A basic lack of capacity to cope with existing demand within
the professionals and services concerned may result in an inability or
unwillingness to consider a change which in the short term will require
further commitment of time. Separate accountability requirements for
budgets, and different priorities for the deployment of resources, can
make it difficult for joint investment and sharing of risk.

Professional barriers often contribute to fragmented care.
These are usually easier to see in other professionals than
within our social work peers. Drawing on the evidence in the
chapter, what barriers to integration have you seen displayed
by social work teams that you have worked in? Reflect on
the influences that may have caused these and what would
support more collaborative practices in the future.

Note

1. Frailty refers to a dynamic state affecting an individual who experiences loss in one or more domains of human functioning (physical, psychological, social). This loss is influenced by a range of variables that increase the risk of adverse outcomes (Looman et al. 2016).

Further resources

Economic and Social Research Council www.esrc.ukri.org

The UK's largest organisation for funding research on economic and social issues. It supports independent, high quality research which has an impact on business, the public sector and civil society.

European Observatory www.euro.who.int/en/about-us/partners/observatory

The European Observatory on Health Systems and Policies supports and promotes evidence-based health policy making through comprehensive and rigorous analysis of the dynamics of health care systems in Europe. The website includes news items, policy briefs and summaries and the BRIDGE series of key lessons and best practice to inform health policy makers and to foster evidence into practice.

International Journal of Integrated Care www.ijic.org

The *International Journal of Integrated Care* (IJIC) is an online, open-access, peer-reviewed scientific journal that publishes original articles in the field of integrated care on a continuous basis.

National Institute for Health Research www.nihr.ac.uk

Major funder of health and care research which seeks to translate discoveries into practical products, treatments, devices and procedures. An excellent source of the latest primary research and evidence reviews.

NSPCC www.nspcc.org.uk/services-and-resources

The NSPCC provides the latest research, child protection statistics, leaflets, practical guidance, briefings and evaluations that share what the NSPCC has learned from its services for children and families.

References

Atkinson, M., Jones, M., & Lamont, E. (2007). *Multi-agency working and its implications for practice*. Reading: CfBT Education Trust. Available at: www.nfer.ac.uk/multi-agency-working-and-its-implications-for-practice-a-review-of-the-literature (downloaded 05.11.2018)

Auschra, C. (2018). Barriers to the integration of care in inter-organisational settings: a literature review. *International Journal of Integrated Care*, *18*(1), 5, 1–14.

Baxter, S., Johnson, M., Chambers, D., Sutton, A., Goyder, E., & Booth, A. (2018). The effects of integrated care: a systematic review of UK and international evidence. *BMC Health Services Research*, *18*(1), 350.

Braye, S., & Preston-Shoot, M. (2017). *Learning from Serious Adult Reviews: a report from the London Safeguarding Adults Board*. Available at: http://londonadass.org.uk/wp-content/uploads/2014/12/London-SARs-Report-Final-Version.pdf (downloaded 05.11.2018)

Cameron, A., Lart, R., Bostock, L., & Coomber, C. (2014). Factors that promote and hinder joint and integrated working between health and social care services: a review of research literature. *Health & Social Care in the Community*, *22*(3), 225–233.

Care Inspectorate. (2016). *Learning from Significant Case Reviews in Scotland*. Available at: www.careinspectorate.com/images/documents/3352/Learning%20from%20Significant%20Case%20Reviews%20in%20Scotland%202012%20-%202015.pdf (downloaded 05.11.2018)

Damery, S., Flanagan, S., & Combes, G. (2016). Does integrated care reduce hospital activity for patients with chronic diseases? An umbrella review of systematic reviews. *BMJ Open, 6*(11), e011952.

Goodwin, N. (2016). Understanding and evaluating the implementation of integrated care: a 'three pipe' problem. *International Journal of Integrated Care, 16*(4), 19.

Hujala, A., Taskinen, H., & Rissanen, S. (2016). *How to support integration to promote care for people with multimorbidity in Europe?* World Health Organization, Regional Office for Europe. Available at: www.euro.who.int/__data/assets/pdf_file/0008/337589/PB_26.pdf

Looman, W. M., Fabbricotti, I. N., de Kuyper, R., & Huijsman, R. (2016). The effects of a pro-active integrated care intervention for frail community-dwelling older people: a quasi-experimental study with the GP-practice as single entry point. *BMC Geriatrics, 16*(1), 43.

Martínez-González, N. A., Berchtold, P., Ullman, K., Busato, A., & Egger, M. (2014). Integrated care programmes for adults with chronic conditions: a meta-review. *International Journal for Quality in Health Care, 26*(5), 561–570.

McLaughlan, H., & Teater, B. (2017). *Evidence-informed practice for social work.* Maidenhead: Open University Press/McGraw Hill.

Miller, R., Williams, I., Allen, K., & Glasby, J. (2014). Evidence, insight, or intuition? Investment decisions in the commissioning of prevention services for older people. *Journal of Care Services Management, 7*(4), 119–127.

Nolte, E., & Pitchforth, E. (2014). *What is the evidence on the economic impacts of integrated care?* Available at: www.euro.who.int/__data/assets/pdf_file/0019/251434/What-is-the-evidence-on-the-economic-impacts-of-integrated-care.pdf   (downloaded 05.11.2018)

NSPCC. (2013) *Domestic violence: learning from case reviews.* Available at: www.nspcc.org.uk/preventing-abuse/child-protection-system/case-reviews/learning/domestic-abuse/ (downloaded 28.08.2018)

NSPCC. (2016). *Summary of risk factors and learning for improved practice when working with deaf and disabled children*. Available at: www.nspcc.org.uk/preventing-abuse/child-protection-system/case-reviews/learning/deaf-disabled-children/ (downloaded 05.11.2018)

NSPCC. (2017). *Harmful sexual behaviour: learning from case reviews*. Available at: www.nspcc.org.uk/preventing-abuse/child-protection-system/case-reviews/learning/harmful-sexual-behaviour/ (downloaded 28.08.2018)

NSPCC. (2018). *Case review process in UK nations*. Available at: https://learning.nspcc.org.uk/case-reviews/process-in-each-uk-nation/ (downloaded 05.11.2018)

Preston-Shoot, M. (2018). Learning from safeguarding adult reviews on self-neglect: addressing the challenge of change. *The Journal of Adult Protection, 20*(2), 78–92.

Rummery, K. (2009). Healthy partnerships, healthy citizens? An international review of partnerships in health and social care and patient/user outcomes. *Social Science & Medicine, 69*(12), 1797–1804.

Seaton, C. L., Holm, N., Bottorff, J. L., Jones-Bricker, M., Errey, S., Caperchione, C. M., ... Healy, T. (2018). Factors that impact the success of interorganizational health promotion collaborations: a scoping review. *American Journal of Health Promotion, 32*(4), 1095–1109.

WHO. (2015). *People-centred and integrated health services: an overview of the evidence*. Available at: www.who.int/servicedeliverysafety/areas/people-centred-care/evidence-overview/en/ (downloaded 05.11.2018).

5 Integrating around individuals

Welfare services in the United Kingdom provide a rich but often incoherent and incomplete range of support for people and their families. There is a bewildering array of sectors and services that may be relevant which could be provided by public, voluntary and/or private organisations. Research repeatedly highlights that people find it difficult to identify the options that are potentially available to them. Information on local services is rarely available through a single source and when there are identified contact points it is rare for these to be comprehensive and fully up to date. Professionals will know services that they have regular contact with but also suffer from limited engagement with many services and insufficient time to investigate all potential options. Furthermore, people may be looking for support at a time in their life when they are experiencing a deterioration or even crisis in their personal situations. This can mean that they have limited time, energy or resilience in researching what is available. Accessing potential opportunities can then be an exhausting and confusing process in which people have to submit various types of information in alternative formats. This will then be compared against eligibility criteria based on factors such as age, geography and condition which may result in them not being suitable. And when support is provided there is no guarantee that there will be any communication between services to ensure that their interventions work together to provide the most value for the people concerned.

The main aim of integrated care is to ensure that people and their families experience coherent support that is focused on their needs and aspirations. It is therefore understandable that many of the approaches that have been deployed to facilitate integrated care focus on the direct services which people receive. In this chapter we will consider four such approaches. All of these seek to help people to make sense of what support is available, to enable them to make informed decisions about what services they access, and to experience a coordinated package of support. This includes improving people's connection with resources within the voluntary and community sector.

> From your practice experience, identify a person and/or family with complex needs who have reported that they had experienced more integrated care (if you cannot think of one who has explicitly reported such an experience then think of a person and/or family who you would consider as likely to do so). What were the elements of their support package that will have contributed to their positive experience?

Care coordination

Coordination is an important element of quality care and support being provided within an organisation. Staff within a care home have to make sure that they have successfully relayed relevant information to the on-coming shift, and clinical specialists within a hospital must share their diagnosis and treatment plans for someone who has been admitted with complex health needs. Our focus here though is on coordination between agencies. This will be necessary to support *vertical integration* which is sometimes referred to as 'sequential' coordination. It is also relevant to *horizontal integration*, which is sometimes referred to as 'parallel' coordination (Øvretveit 2011). Coordination is seen to support people in experiencing 'continuity' in their care. This is commonly highlighted by people as being an important aspect of quality of care and relates to feeling that there is a 'continuous caring relationship' from professionals. In the past this may have been provided by a single professional but for people with multiple conditions or issues it will require engagement with multiple professionals and services (Gulliford et al. 2006). The WHO describes four domains of continuity – interpersonal, longitudinal, management and informational (see Box 5.1).

Box 5.1 Four domains of continuity (WHO 2018)

Interpersonal continuity: the subjective experience of the caring relationship between a patient and his or her health care professional

Longitudinal continuity: a history of interaction with the same health care professional in a series of discrete episodes

Management continuity: effective collaboration of teams across care boundaries to provide seamless care

Informational continuity: the availability of clinical and psychosocial information at all encounters with professionals.

Many people and their families effectively undertake their own care coordination. Some will have the skills and confidence to liaise and negotiate with professionals. The role often falls to family carers which can add to their responsibilities and the many demands on their time. When someone's situation is more complex, and/or if they do not have the capacity or ability then a more formal coordination of their care may be required. The National Coalition on Care Coordination in the USA is a network of organisations that seeks to improve the quality of care people receive from the health and social care sector. It describes care coordination as follows:

> a person-centred, assessment-based, interdisciplinary approach to integrating health care and social support services in a cost-effective manner in which an individual's needs and preferences are assessed, a comprehensive care plan is developed, and services are managed and monitored by an evidence-based process which typically involves a designated lead care coordinator.
>
> (National Coalition on Care Coordination 2011, p1)

Table 5.1 Elements of care coordination (Sheaff et al. 2015)

Element	Domain of continuity
A care coordinator combines the support from different professionals and services into a coherent process that meets the person's needs. This support is documented in a care plan which delineates between the responsibilities and activities of the professionals and services	Management
The person can access the identified support with no barriers or gaps and these services understand and respond to what is important to them. This will sometimes require active facilitation by the care coordinator	Management Interpersonal
The care coordinator maintains an ongoing relationship with the person	Interpersonal Longitudinal
The care plan is shared between the professionals and services, and with the person	Informational
The care coordinator reviews the person's circumstances and, if these change, alters the resources or services offered	Management
There is on-going transfer of information between the professionals and services and/or shared access to electronic records	Informational

Coordination is seen to involve a number of elements which support different domains of continuity (Table 5.1).

How could care coordination provide more integrated care?

Care coordination seeks to address the common lack of communication and organisation between agencies and professionals. It sits above the assessment and interventions undertaken by individual services and introduces a new set of processes to ensure that they connect around the person. Identifying a designated coordinator means that it is clear who is responsible for leading on the integration process and through whom the various professionals can keep others informed. The coordinator also provides a point of contact for the person and their family with whom they can raise any concerns.

Care coordination in mental health

People with severe and enduring mental health problems may have periods in their lives in which they are in receipt of support from multiple professionals and services. If their mental health starts to decline, then they may benefit from intensive support to avoid entering into a time of crisis. If they are admitted to a crisis unit or into hospital, then there will be a need to plan their support on discharge to ensure that they have somewhere to live and the right health and social care package to maintain their mental wellbeing in the community. Outside of crisis periods, it can often be difficult for people to secure employment and develop social networks due to a lack of confidence and discrimination within mainstream sectors. People may therefore benefit from having support from community agencies with understanding of the challenges that people with mental health problems can face.

All of nations within the UK have introduced a care coordination process for people accessing mental health services. The Care Programme Approach (CPA) was introduced in 1990 in England as a joint circular between NHS organisations and local authorities. Initial guidance introduced the role of 'key worker' to oversee arrangements for monitoring and review, and keeping in close contact with the person. Key workers could be any of the health and social care professionals working within mental health. Subsequent policy directives refined the approach, with the 'modernising the care programme' guidance being produced in 1999. This introduced two levels of CPA – standard and enhanced (Box 5.2). People eligible for *standard* CPA may only have received one specialist service but would still have a care plan and review. Their level of risk was low, and they were seen to have the skills and motivation to engage with services. *Enhanced* CPA related to those with complex needs and multiple supports who were more at risk of losing contact with their services. The key worker role was subsequently renamed care coordinator with recognition that implementation would require support and change across the organisations. In 2008, there was then a move away from the two levels. This was on the basis that research had highlighted that for people at the standard level there was too great an emphasis on managing the process rather than the end goal of providing more person-centred care. From that point on CPA in England would only to be used to describe the approach used to assess, plan, review and co-ordinate people who have 'complex characteristics'. The guidance emphasised that it was an '"approach", rather than just a system, because the way that these elements are carried out is as important as the actual tasks themselves' (DH 2008, p11).

Box 5.2 Enhanced and standard Care Programme Approach (DH 1999)

People on standard CPA: they require the support or intervention of one agency or discipline or they require only low key support from more than one agency or discipline; they are more able to self-manage their mental health problems; they have an active informal support network; they pose little danger to themselves or others; they are more likely to maintain appropriate contact with services.

People on enhanced CPA are likely to have some of the following characteristics: they have multiple care needs, including housing, employment etc, requiring interagency coordination; they are only willing to co-operate with one professional or agency but they have multiple care needs; they may be in contact with a number of agencies (including the Criminal Justice System); they are likely to require more frequent and intensive interventions, perhaps with medication management; they are more likely to have mental health problems co-existing with other problems such as substance misuse; they are more likely to be at risk of harming themselves or others; they are more likely to disengage with services.

A two-tiered approach to CPA was introduced in Wales in 2003 with a requirement for care coordinators to be identified for people receiving 'enhanced' CPA (Welsh Assembly Government 2003). The comprehensive multi-disciplinary care plan was based on a holistic assessment of need and include detailed contingency and crisis plans. The Mental Health (Wales) Measure 2010 legislation introduced a new legal requirement for all people in receipt of secondary mental health services to have a care coordinator and a 'proportionate and holistic care and treatment plan' (p1). The associated code of practice (Welsh Assembly Government 2012) contains detailed guidance about the role of the care coordinator and the process for selecting these by the mental health service providers. This should be a combination of the professional having the right experience, skills and training, their relationship with the person and their ability to meet the language and communication needs. Furthermore, there should be consideration of the person's preference and choice, any conflicts of interest and the professional having sufficient workload capacity. There is an emphasis throughout on the care coordinator working in collaboration with the person to ensure that they are fully informed and that the care plan reflects their perspectives. Care coordinators are also expected to take all practicable steps to consult with carers and/or those with parental responsibility for the person.

The Mental Health (Wales) Measure 2010 places a further duty on Welsh Ministers to review the implementation and impact of the care coordination arrangements. The review published in 2015 reported that 86 per cent of people receiving secondary mental health services had a valid care and treatment plan. A survey in one health board area of 200 people supported by community mental health teams suggested that many of them had positive experiences (Box 5.3). However, the approach was not being consistently implemented to the required standard across Wales. For example, people frequently reported that clinicians were only focusing on medication despite there being an expectation that they would encompass eights aspects of people's lives (including accommodation, parenting and education). Social workers were seen as being most professionally qualified to take on the holistic role of care coordinator but that it was more common in practice for nurses to take on this responsibility (Welsh Assembly Government 2015). The difficulties of consistency reflect the experience of the CPA in England in which it is implementation rather than agreeing the framework that has been the challenge (Goodwin & Lawton-Smith 2010). Research of care coordination across Wales and England also suggests that there is a difference between how such work 'is imagined' and how it such work 'is done' (Hannigan et al. 2018). Their interviews reflect a commitment by the coordinators to be relational in their approach but that much of their time is spent completing paperwork (which often changed) and meeting connected targets.

Box 5.3 Survey responses from people regarding care coordination in Wales (Welsh Assembly Government 2016)

- Over 91 per cent stated they had a Care and Treatment Plan (CTP) and an equivalent percentage knew their care coordinator
- 88 per cent of people understood the purpose of their CTP
- 92 per cent felt involved in the development of their CTP or were not involved because they chose not to be
- Over 83 per cent either had their families or carers involved in the development of their CTP or did not wish them to be
- 94 per cent felt that staff involved in CTP were understanding/supportive
- 89 per cent of service uses were satisfied with their CTP and 88% felt their received care matched their CTP
- 54 per cent of people were offered their CTP in Welsh or language of their choice.

Care coordination for children and young people with a disability

The Children and Families Act 2014 includes responsibilities for local authorities in England to ensure integration between special educational needs, health and social care provision where this would promote the wellbeing of children or young people or improve the quality of provision. The legislation introduced a new process for Education, Health and Care assessment and planning. The purpose of this process is to establish and record the views, interests and aspirations of the parents and child or young person; provide a full description of their needs; establish outcomes based on their needs and aspirations; and specify the provision required and how education, health and care services will work together. The Code of Practice expects key working to be available for those undergoing an assessment and plan but recognises that there are different ways that the connected functions could be provided (see Box 5.4).

Box 5.4 Four functional areas of key working within the Education, Health and Care planning process (Hill et al. 2014)

Emotional and practical support:

- a trusting relationship to build family resilience
- enabling decision making including use of personal budgets
- advocating for a child, young person and their family

Information:

- on local interpretation of national policy
- options for provision

Coordination

- single point of contact for the family
- coordinating involvement of professionals and services
- facilitating multi-agency meetings

Assessment and planning

- coordinating a single process
- drafting elements of the plan

A pathfinder programme was established to inform the national changes to the special educational needs assessment and statement framework. Twenty sites involving 31 local authorities were funded from October 2011 to September 2014 to trial approaches for implementing the common assessment process, the single Education, Health and Care plan, and personal budgets. Pathfinders deployed two models in respect of key working (Table 5.2). A *single person model*, in which one professional was given responsibility for overseeing the process, or a *multi-person model*, in which two or more professionals took on key working responsibilities. The latter involved two roles – a *coordinator* who meets with the family, organises the multi-agency meetings and draws up the non-statutory aspects of the plan, and a *lead professional* (or professionals) who works with other disciplines to review evidence, draft the statutory aspects of the plan and calculate the resources that are required. In some areas both models were deployed and the most appropriate one selected dependent on the intensity of need and/or age of the child or young person.

Families in the pathfinder areas were more likely than those in non-pathfinder comparators to report that they had a key worker. They were slightly more likely to say that they had confidence in the key worker's ability to arrange the necessary support (68 per cent to 62 per cent). A key worker was described as one factor that contributed to families feeling better informed about potential services. Once the plan was in place there was often a change in how coordination was provided with many families then not aware if they even had a key worker. At this point responsibility often transferred to school staff who knew the child or young person, but families were not sure that they had the capacity or skills to liaise with and influence the wider professional group. For both models, professionals reported experiencing greater pressure on their time due to the requirement to co-produce the plan with families and in securing timely input from all other professionals and services. Not all of those asked to undertake key working duties appeared to have the required skills. Bespoke training was therefore required to ensure a commonality of approach and a consistency in quality.

Table 5.2 Comparison of two key working models (Hill et al. 2014)

Model	Benefits	Drawbacks
Single person	One point of contact for family Ownership by a single person facilitates coordination Families identify one person as holding responsibility	One person needs authority and capability to influence others Single person needs a wide skill set and sufficient capacity Can be emotionally demanding and/or isolating for key worker
Multi-person	Team of people brings variety of skills Family can have greater choice over which professional they engage with most Professionals involved can provide each other with emotional support	Has to be efficient process for sharing of information Can be confusion if family in contact with multiple professionals Professionals need similar understanding of key working and their respective roles

Discussion

There is considerable evidence that lower quality outcomes result from under-coordination of care and this is particularly problematic at key times of change in someone's life stage, support package or location of care (Øvretveit 2011). Research also suggests that for some transitions, social circumstances and health conditions, better coordination can improve outcomes and ensure that resources are used more effectively. There is though substantial evidence that coordination does not improve outcomes or efficiency for all populations and in all contexts. A particular issue in relation to the latter is that a care coordination programme designed to respond to fragmentation in one area may not be simply replicated in another locality. Introducing care coordination can take many years due to the need to skill up the relevant professionals, ensure that the necessary governance and information systems are in place and provide required information for people and their families (Goodwin et al. 2013). Many professionals will also require convincing that this is a role that they should undertake as it can be perceived that it detracts them for deploying their specialist skills. Their managers may also need convincing that this a priority for their already busy teams when it involves organising the work of others. Ensuring that professionals have the capacity to undertake the role is essential if coordination is going to have a positive impact.

Local area coordination

Local Area Coordination (LAC) was developed in Western Australia in the late 1980s. It sought to facilitate self-sufficiency for people with a disability and their families living in remote areas due to a lack of formal services in such communities. It has since been introduced in other states in Australia (and is a component of the recent National Disability Insurance Scheme), New Zealand, Scotland, Wales and England. It was also piloted for a short time in Northern Ireland. Whilst it is more commonly been offered to people with a disability there are also examples of LAC being available to wider populations who have a need and/or vulnerability. It has a strong value base arising from the social model of disability which emphasises the rights of people to be self-determining, to be included in mainstream society and to have opportunities to develop as individuals (see Box 5.5). Eddie Bartnik, who founded LAC, summarises its approach as follows:

> the reform was built on an assumption that people with disabilities are not just passive recipients of services. Along with their families, friends and local communities, they have expertise, natural authority and assets that can maximize the impact of resources and improve outcomes. The reform also emphasizes the transformative effects of shifting power, resources and accountability for outcomes to a partnership between government and people, where together problems are defined and solutions designed and implemented.
>
> (Bartnik 2010, p118)

Box 5.5 The principles of Local Area Coordination (Broad 2012)

Citizenship – with all its responsibilities and opportunities

Relationships – the importance of personal networks and families

Information – supporting decision making

Gifts – all that individuals, families and communities bring

Expertise – the knowledge held by people and their families

Leadership – the right to plan, choose and control your own life and support

Services – as a back up to natural support

LAC involves an individual (the local area coordinator) being available to people living in an identified small local area as informal point of contact for advice, discussion and support. The emphasis is on access to the service being open rather than tightly bound by criteria and referral processes. There is not a set range of services that can be accessed via the coordinator. Instead they work with the individual and their family to build a bespoke network of support. The quality of the relationships between the coordinator, the individual and (if appropriate) the family is seen as central. This should be a partnership, rather than a professional–client relationship, with the individual having the ultimate say over what, if any, action they take. Coordinators should be embedded in their local communities so that they can become familiar with all of the resources that could be relevant. They may seek to encourage the creation of new local assets if there appears to be a significant gap in the support available.

How could local area coordination provide more integrated care?

LAC starts with the individual and what matters to them. There is no assumption that formal or indeed informal services will be required, but if support would seem beneficial then a package should be built around the individual. The emphasis is on working with the person to construct a tailored package of support. This is a different starting point to what people often experience with traditional services in which there is a set menu of support or interventions that are available. The local area coordinator will be available if the identified supports do not work in practice. In traditional models when someone is 'referred on' on then their 'case' is often 'closed' meaning that they have to start the process again if this is not suitable.

Local area coordination in Thurrock

Thurrock is a local authority to the East of London. Its interest in LAC began in 2012 as part of a broader programme to improve the health and wellbeing of older and vulnerable people. This was centred around hospitable, age-friendly communities and providing more choices regarding when and how people lived. LAC was selected as it was seen to build partnerships with (Snitch 2013):

- people – who may be vulnerable, isolated or excluded due to age, frailty, disability or mental health needs to help them stay strong and connected and find non-service solutions to issues wherever possible
- communities – to help make them more welcoming, inclusive and mutually supportive
- services – to promote a simpler, more connected system, better outcomes for local people and services that are more personal, flexible and local.

It was introduced in three localities initially, but due to enthusiasm from other stakeholders was quickly broadened out across the authority. Funding was provided by the adult social care management team (on the basis that it would reduce demands on their service), the Fire and Rescue Service (as it would support their community engagement work), Public Health (due to the potential for improvements in people's health and wellbeing) and the Better Care Fund (to reduce admissions to hospital). Two levels of support are available through LAC – level 1 was open to anyone and involved the provision of information and/or limited support, and level 2 which was accessible to people who are vulnerable and involved a longer-term relationship. Coordinators are recruited through a citizen led process in which community groups are active participants in the selection of candidates (see Box 5.6).

Box 5.6 Citizen-led recruitment in Thurrock

The emphasis in selecting coordinators was on recruiting people with the right values rather than on those from particular professions. A standard advert did not result in enough good applications, so a more creative approach was used. A further advert was run and everyone who expressed an interest (over 100 people) were invited to attend an all-day event. Community representatives were placed on four tables and the candidates circulated around these groups to respond to set questions. These included identifying on a map what community resources that they were aware of and discussing 'what I love about Thurrock is'. Candidates were scored by the groups and this was used to shortlist 16 people to participate in a formal interview.

An independent assessment of the social value of LAC in Thurrock was published in 2015. People who had accessed the service described feeling more confident and less isolated. Many had been able to access new training, development and volunteering opportunities and others had more sustainable tenancies. The report estimates that for every £1 invested in LAC there would be £4 of social value created (Kingfishers 2015). A separate evaluation undertaken by Thurrock Council highlights the benefits of LAC for some of the individuals concerned (see Box 5.7).

Box 5.7 Impact of local area coordination for one person, Mr R (Snitch 2013)

Mr R was a 69-year-old man, with a history of depression. He had made suicide attempts which required admission to hospital. There is limited family support and although physically healthy, Mr R was quite isolated and wanted to look at local facilities where he could make friends.

The LAC took time to get to know Mr R, to find out what was important to him and explore what a good life looked like to him. Mr R's key priority was to get out of the flat where he spent most of his time, as this contributed to his depression. He expressed a desire to help other people and to make more friends as well as wanting to feel safe, secure and confident. The LAC supported Mr R to explore family support from Ngage (a voluntary organisation supporting communities in Thurrock) and this resulted in Mr R becoming a volunteer driver three days a week with the Royal Volunteering Service. He completed a course in Computers for Absolute Beginners at Thurrock Adult College to enable access to social networks. He is also now able to provide support to others in his community, including one woman with agoraphobia and another who was unable to leave his home due to ulcerated legs.

Local community coordination in Bridgend

The Western Bay Health and Social Programme in South-West Wales was developed by the local health board and three local authorities to promote prevention and wellbeing from a citizen-centred perspective. Its aims include 'integrating services more effectively for the benefit of service users and carers'. As part of the programme, Neath Port Talbot County Borough Council and the City and County of Swansea introduced Local Area Coordination.

Bridgend County Borough Council decided to use the core prin-ciples of LAC to launch Local Community Coordination. As well as providing advice and support to individuals there is a stronger emphasis than for many LAC services on undertaking community development. This began in 2015 with a team of three coordinators and a support officer. The coordinators support a population of 10–15,000 with areas being selected on the basis of high levels of deprivation and unemployment and poor levels of health and well-being. For example, projects that the coordinators have been involved with include:

- Strictly Cinema – this project not only organises film showings but also offers meals and tea dances to enhance social opportunities.
- IPads Project – technology sessions have been run at a day hospital to improve older people's ability to engage with social media.
- Try it, Do it – held in four venues, these sessions bring together small groups of older people to socialise in order to grow their social networks. One session for older men was so successful that it grew into a separate social enterprise (Shedquarters) enabling the members to buy their own allotment.
- Creativity for Wellbeing – this is a social prescribing project in which the general practice can refer people to creative activities led by an arts therapist.

The Local Community Coordinators promote these activities through an accessible website – www.lcc.community/#about.

Discussion

An evidence review of LAC in Australia (Chadbourne 2003) con-cluded that evaluation suggests that 'positive [impacts] of LAC can be regarded as continuous, enduring, long term and consist-ent over time' (ibid., p1). Positive outcomes for individuals included improved mental wellbeing, enhanced self-sufficiency, more choice and control, and accessing a diverse and individual-ised range of support options. Broader impacts included improved inclusion of people with disabilities in the community, decreased use of residential care and a better use of resources. The review suggests that the methodology of the evaluations was generally sound, although it does call for more objective and crit-ical research to be carried out. The University of Stirling under-took an evaluation of the implementation of LAC in 24 Scottish local authorities. There was sufficient evidence of positive impact that they were able to conclude that

> individuals gained improved access to services, support and information as a result of their contact with LACs. In some cases, inter-agency cooperation was enhanced and commu-nity capacity building was seen as an important aspect of the overall work of LACs.
>
> (Stalker et al. 2007, p125)

However, these outcomes were diminished in those areas in which the approach was not implemented thoroughly. They found that there was considerable variation in how the approach was being realised in practice, with the key elements of an open access system and focus on community development being lost in many areas. This was in part due to the difficulties of combin-ing LAC within the established pattern of service delivery in Scot-land. This was a barrier in Northern Ireland along with a lack of support from policy makers and a difficult financial climate leading to general cost cutting in public services (Vincent 2010). The Local Area Coordination Network in England and Wales strongly believes that implementing LAC 'is challenging because it requires changing everything' (Broad 2015, p13). This includes fundamen-tally reviewing the relationship between the welfare state and its citizens, the role of existing professionals and the purpose of joint working.

Social prescribing

Whilst formal health care services have an important role to play in helping people respond to short term illnesses and longer-term health conditions, there are many aspects of health and wellbeing for which they are not that effective or resourced. They are often limited for example in their ability to support people to make life-style choices such as to eat healthier diets or take more exercise. Health care struggles to address the underlying social issues that contribute to people having poor health and wellbeing, such as housing, employment, domestic violence, fear of crime and loneli-ness. Social workers understand the importance of these factors on people's lives but due to limited capacity are generally restricted to working with people for whom these have reached a crisis point in their lives. Most of the support that is available to support people with these aspects of their lives and to be more proactive in maintaining their wellbeing is therefore provided by the voluntary and community sector. However, health care ser-vices, including general practice, have traditionally been poor at understanding what such support is available in their local com-munity and how someone can access it.

Box 5.8 Common elements of social prescribing (NHS England 2016a)

The central role of an asset-based approach to development

A stronger focus on wellness not illness

An emphasis on the importance of personal choice and con-trol in achieving and maintaining wellbeing

The need to re-imagine future workforce development and training needs with new kinds of bridging roles

The value of this approach in terms of the potential to con-tribute to real transformation of health and care systems through joint endeavour

---

Social prescribing is an umbrella term for approaches that seek to facilitate people drawing on the resources that are available in their local communities (Box 5.8). It has been introduced on a small scale from the 1990s but in recent years has gained prominence in all the home nations of the UK and internationally. For example, the Cabinet Secretary for Health, Wellbeing and Sport wrote to all health boards in 2017 that the Welsh government is 'championing social prescribing'. It is one of the ten high-impact changes recommended by NHS England (2016b) to release pressure in primary care. There is no one model as such, but there are a common set of principles (see Box 5.8). Social prescribing generally involves a link worker of some description talking with a person about what support may be of help and then connecting them with appropriate organisations. The link worker may be based in general practices and/or community locations, and will often (but not exclusively) be employed by a voluntary

---

**Box 5.9 Types of social prescribing services
(NHS England 2016a)**

Providing information and advice on legal issues, education, housing and welfare benefits

Reading material that supports people to better understand and manage their condition (bibliotherapy)

Engaging with the natural environment through for example gardening, walking outdoors or a conservation project (eco-therapy)

Opportunity to create their own art or meet others with an interest in cultural activities

General exercise programmes or those developed for specific conditions such as recovering from a stroke

Volunteering for community projects to contribute to the community and strengthen their own sense of worth and social networks

Learning through adult education classes or more informal sources of gaining new knowledge and developing skills

organisation. People may be able to access the service themselves, or may need a referral (a 'social prescription') from a
health or social care professional. There should not be a
restricted menu of community resources. The services suggested will depend on their needs, and the offer available from
within their local community (see Box 5.9). As well as promoting
better outcomes for individuals, social prescribing is potentially a
way to divert activity from general practice to other services. It
has been estimated that between 15–20 per cent of patients
consult their GP for a social rather than health issue (Torjesen
2016).

How could social prescribing provide more integrated care?

In the past it has been difficult for professionals, people and
their families to recognise all of the community resources that
are available. Social prescribing could act as the bridge
between health care services and community-based resources.
If the 'prescription' results in people growing their social network, then this can further increase their knowledge of resources and give them confidence in approaching other
organisations. It can raise the awareness of professionals of
community options and so they may suggest a service directly
to an individual.

Social prescribing in Torfaen

Torfaen County Borough Council and the Torfaen Neighbourhood
Care Networks developed a social prescribing project in South
Wales. Two social prescribers were based for half a day a week
in each of 13 general practices. Appointments were booked by
the practice staff and the social prescriber could access the
health notes of the patients. The person is encouraged to take

their time with the prescriber to enable them to tell their whole story so 45 minutes is booked for each appointment (with flexibility to run over if necessary).

Box 5.10 Example of impacts of social prescribing for one person

H was referred to the social prescriber by a concerned relative. There had been some issues with the payment of his Employment Support Allowance (ESA), he was not opening his mail or leaving his home and needed to see the GP but would not make an appointment. On initial visit the social prescriber and Communities First Financial Inclusion Officer were concerned, amongst other things, for his mental wellbeing.

The presenting needs of lack of food, re-instatement of benefits and accessing the GP were supported and focus shifted to the underlying needs and how H could resolve them. Within days H had gone from someone who would not answer the door, the phone or open his mail to someone who was re-arranging his own appointments, organising transport and arranging for a family member to undertake some domestic tasks. By providing the support to remove the immediate stresses, the social prescriber had enabled the capacity within H to support himself. This had a positive impact on his self-esteem which promotes his ability to cope. He has now been allocated a support worker from Gwalia to continue his journey to wellness.

The first year report of the Torfaen project (ABUHB 2017) states that 41 per cent of people were connected with organisations that could support with financial and housing issues, 17 per cent to mental wellbeing services and 9 per cent to housing support services. Many of the people referred to social prescribing found difficulty in engaging with other people and some suffered from severe mental health problems. This meant that the prescribers had to support them in their initial engagement with community resources rather than simply providing them with the contact details (Primary Care Hub 2018).

Links worker programme in Glasgow

General Practitioners at the Deep End is a network of general practices serving the 100 most deprived populations in Scotland. Facilitated by the University of Glasgow, it has provided many insights into the lives of people living in such communities and ways in which primary care services can provide better support. The network identified that social disadvantage was main contributor to people seeking help but that general practitioners did not have the time or connections with community resources to respond appropriately (GPDE 2010). This has led to a series of projects exploring opportunities to connect primary care and the voluntary sector. Scottish government has funded the Links Worker Programme for at least five years to work with individuals in seven general practices in Glasgow who may benefit from connection with community resources. The programme is also seeking to help general practices to become more holistic in their approach. Community Links Practitioners are employed by a voluntary sector organisation (Health and Social Care Alliance Scotland) and then based in the general practice. As well as working with individuals, they will support the practice team in developing a plan to transform their thinking based on seven capacities (see Box 5.11). Each practice has received a small development grant to fund related activities. Community Links Practitioners are also engaging with community resources to help them become more accessible to people who may be referred from primary care.

Box 5.11 Capacities for general practices to engage with communities (Health & Social Care Alliance 2018)

1. Team wellbeing
   A primary care team that's in survival mode, or feels overwhelmed by demands, cannot effectively offer patients support. The business plan must demonstrate how the team plans to support staff wellbeing and create an environment where there is enough time for staff to listen and advise people.
2. Shared learning
   GP practices need to have protected time for shared learning, access to educational resources and the opportunity to share stories.
3. Awareness
   Staff need to be able to identify people who would benefit from information or support, to have a wider understanding of the social context of illness.
4. Intelligence
   Practices need to be able to gather information, to curate that information and have efficient and accessible processes for people to receive this information.
5. Signposting
   Practices need to be able to routinely provide information about local support to people.
6. Problem solving
   Links Practitioners have capacity to work with people to identify and solve problems.
7. Network building
   Primary care teams need to develop an extensive network of personal relationships in their local community.

The evaluation by the University of Glasgow compared the seven practices involved with similar practices not implementing this approach (Mercer et al. 2017). They found that patients appreciated the listening approach taken by the Community Links Practitioners and this made them feel valued. Some were able to better manage their health having visited the community resource, but others did not find it of any benefit. This was reflected in the quantitative analysis that found no statistically different patient outcomes or use of health care services. Practices varied considerably in their ability and willingness to undertake the wider changes that will lead to their wider team being more holistic and community orientated in their work. The programme has produced a series of learning guides to share its evolving experience and knowledge.

Primary care navigation for people with dementia in Gateshead

The Oxford Terrace and Rawling Road Medical Group provides general practice services across two sites. As well as doctors, the service employs occupational therapists, practice nurses and a nurse practitioner. It had also developed good working relationships with other agencies including social care, mental health and midwifery. They identified that they had a higher than average proportion of patients with dementia and that they were more likely to experience unplanned admissions to hospital. They and their family carers generally had a lower satisfaction with the support provided.

Rather than engage with an external voluntary organisation the practice decided to skill up two of their health care assistants to provide better navigation for people with dementia and their family carers. On-line training and peer support was provided to the assistants to improve their understanding of dementia and the community resources that were available. This was important as they reported at the beginning of the project being nervous about taking on the role and what would be expected of them. They would regularly contact people via the telephone or visiting their home, and arranged events in which people could meet others who had developed or were caring for someone with dementia. Other professionals in the practice referred people to the navigators and they identified patients they were already working with who could benefit. Through investigating potential options for people, they have been able to build a directory of relevant services.

In the first three months, the navigators connected 43 carers and 20 older people with services. They also developed almost 400 care plans and reviewed the medication of around 90 patients. Hospital admissions fell by up to 80 per cent for these people. The navigators also reported feeling happier working for the practice and being more confident in their role (Deloites & NAPC 2017).

Discussion

A systematic review of the evidence for social prescribing identified 15 studies (Bickerdike et al. 2017). These were described as being of small scale and with weak methodologies due to a lack of comparative controls, non-validated measuring tools and insufficient consideration of other contributory factors. Accepting these limitations, six out of the eight studies which reported on patient experience described overall satisfaction of participants. Reduced social isolation and loneliness were also observed. Literacy, confidence, travel practicalities and interest influence people's willingness and ability to engage with the 'prescribed' services. There is insufficient evidence as yet to determine if social prescribing is cost effective (University of York 2015) but one recent review suggests that there are indications that it can have a protective effect on service demand (Polley & Pilkington 2017). The evidence suggests that if well implemented it can support better integration between formal primary care services and community resources. However, it is not yet clear what model of social prescribing works best in what circumstances, and which interventions or support are best when provided by community organisations.

Individual budgets

One of the major developments in recent years in adult social care has been the option for those eligible for public funding to directly manage their own budgets. There are a number of arguments for the introduction of such arrangements. People have a right to be self-determining over their lives which includes how and where any support is provided. A lack of transparency about the funding that they are entitled to receive with professionals making decisions over how this funding is used will detract from this right. People are best placed to identify what matters most to them and their families and therefore should know best how to use the funding available most effectively. There is an economic argument that if people are able to act as 'consumers' in a market of social care then the market will respond to what they want to buy so increasing choice and quality. It is fair to say that there are supporters as well as detractors of polices which seek to promote people managing their own budgets. Concerns relate to the marketisation of social care services, providers becoming financially insecure due to uncertainties over their funding, and governments using the arrangements to introduce reductions in funding. Inequalities could be promoted as those who are more educated and confident are often better able to derive the most benefit from overseeing their eligible funding. Sufficient support is therefore a necessity to ensure that people feel informed and enabled, and that managing their budget is not another stress on them and their families.

Debates about the principle of people holding their own social care budgets will undoubtedly continue. All the home nations have introduced this option under different titles – self-directed support in Scotland and Northern Ireland, and direct payments in England and Wales. Along with the opportunity for individuals and families to receive the money are options to have funding managed by a trusted group of others or for the local authority to retain control but with greater transparency about what the budget is and how it is used. Individual service funds, in which a provider of social care services holds the budget on behalf of the person, is another development. England has gone further than other parts of the UK in relation to such mechanisms through also introducing individual budgets for health care services. This includes funding for support for people with significant ongoing health care needs within their own home or in residential care.

How could individual budgets provide more integrated care?

When people need to draw on multiple sources of public sector support this can amplify a lack of clarity about what they are entitled to and the difficulties in being able to direct how funding is used. Even when people do know what budget is available, it can then be hard to direct how it is used as agencies may only be willing to have resources used in certain ways. Enabling the person to know what budget they are eligible for from different agencies and to have control over how these are used could lead to greater flexibility to respond to their individual situation and needs.

Integrated personal commissioning

The opportunity for people with complex needs to blend the funding provided by health and social care in England was announced in 2014 in the Five Year Forward View. People would be provided details of a 'year of care' budget with options to manage this themselves or with the help of voluntary organisations, local authorities or the NHS. Budgets could include funding from education for children and young people. The Integrated Personal Commissioning Programme selected demonstrator sites to explore how to provide such arrangements for people with complex needs in their area. Nine sites were initially selected in 2015 with another nine 'early adopters' in late 2016 (NHSE 2018). Each of the sites have a focus on one or more of the populations – children and young people with complex needs including those eligible for Education, Health and Care plans; people with multiple long-term conditions particularly older people with frailty; people with learning disabilities with high support needs including those who are in institutional settings or at risk of being placed in these settings; and people with significant mental health needs such as those eligible for the Care Programme Approach or those who use high levels of unplanned care.

Box 5.12 Integrated personal budgets in Lambeth (SCIE 2014)

Integrated personal budgets started in Lambeth in July 2012. The clinical commissioning group and the local authority developed a pooled budget hosted by Lambeth Council. When it is agreed that someone can received funding from this pot then an agreement is reached about what percentage will come respectively from health and social care. Once the budget is set, a worker from the voluntary sector Community Options team will usually work with the individual as a broker to produce a support plan. Community Options is independent of both health and social care services and their workers have a good knowledge of community resources. Examples of things that people have spent their budgets on include: seasonal affective disorder (SAD) lights, gym membership, SKY TV, removal fees and a gravestone. All mental health team staff receive training in support planning (one day) and recovery support planning (one day) and the personalisation coordinator often goes into teams as part of their development.

The initial learning from the demonstrators has led to an emerging framework for implementation (see Table 5.3). This emphasises that much more than a budgetary process is required if people are going to benefit from the new arrangements. The framework recommends that integrated budgets be part of a broader programme that seeks to make care more person centred. This is likely to include enhanced multidisciplinary teams which bring together generalist and specialist professionals from health, social care and other services. The

Table 5.3 Five shifts for integrated personal commissioning (LGA & NHSE 2016)

Element	Description
Proactive coordination of care	A proactive approach to integrating care at individual level around adults, children and young people with complex needs
Community capacity and peer support	A community and peer focus to build knowledge, skills and confidence for self-management
Personalised care and support planning	A different conversation about health and care focused on what is important to each person, through personalised care and support planning
Choice and control	A shift in control over the resources available to people, carers and families, through personal budgets
Personalised commissioning and payment	A wider range of care and support options tailored to individual needs and preferences, through personalised commissioning, contracting and payment

programme report estimates that 5 per cent of the general population could benefit from such an approach.

The initial evaluation highlights that the demonstrator sites have found that implementing the approach is highly complex and requires active support from senior managers due to the complexity and scale of change (Agur et al. 2018). Laying the foundations, such as developing multidisciplinary teams and developing a linked dataset, involved considerable time and resources. This meant that the sites had not made as much progress as they anticipated. Those that had engaged an external organisation to lead on the programme appeared to have made the most progress. A common barrier was that existing funding for many individuals was tied up in a 'block contract' with existing services. There was also a lack of financial systems to allow alternative services to receive payment through an integrated personal budget.

Discussion

Research on personal budgets for only social care and health care services suggests that it can lead to better outcomes for some people in some aspects of their lives. It generally has greater impact on aspects of wellbeing more directly connected with health and social care services, such as a feeling of being in control and flexibility over mode of delivery, than broader aspects such as social inclusion. Research also underlines that most people will need support to take on this responsibility and that without such support, managing a budget can provide added burden and stress to the individual and/or their family carer. Integrated personal budgets bring added complexity. This includes financial elements such as differences in VAT rules between health and social care and the charges that people need to pay for some services in some countries. It also requires closer collaboration between the professionals responsible for supporting the individual and a shared understanding of the purpose (SCIE 2014).

Reflect on people and/or families with complex support packages whom you have supported in your placements or in work. Do you think that any of these approaches (care coordination, local area coordination, social prescribing or individual budgets) would have improved their experience of care? What else could have been changed in or added to their support to provide a more integrated package?

Further resources

Council for Disabled Children https://councilfordisabledchildren.org.uk/about

The Council for Disabled Children is an umbrella body for the disabled children's sector bringing together professionals, practitioners and policy makers.

Health and Social Care Alliance Scotland www.alliance-scotland. org.uk

The Health and Social Care Alliance Scotland brings together over 2,500 members including large, national support providers as well as small, local volunteer-led groups and people who are disabled, living with long-term conditions or providing unpaid care. It leads numerous innovative projects and shares emerging lessons.

International Journal of Care Coordination https://journals. sagepub.com/home/icp

The *International Journal of Care Coordination* provides an international forum for the latest scientific research in care coordination. The journal publishes original articles and opinion pieces for a multidisciplinary audience. Topics include strategies to improve care coordination and latest innovations.

Primary Care One www.primarycareone.wales.nhs.uk/home

The Primary Care One website provides professionals and stakeholders working in, or with an interest in, primary care in Wales with a source of up to date information both nationally and locally. This includes programmes promoting more integrated care.

References

ABUHB. (2017). *Social prescribing in Torfaen: a partnership between North and South Torfaen Neighbourhood Care Networks (NCNs) our learning so far: October 2015–March 2017.* Available at: www.primarycareone.wales.nhs.uk/sitesplus/docu ments/1191/Social%20Prescribing%20in%20Torfaen%20Oct% 2015%20-%20Mar%2017.pdf (downloaded 05.11.2018)

Agur, M., Thom, G., & Baxter, C. (2018). *Summative evaluation of the Integrated Personal Commissioning (IPC) Programme: interim report – process evaluation November 2017*. Available at: www.sqw.co.uk/insights-and-publications/evaluation-of-the-integrated-personal-commissioning-programme/ (downloaded 05.11.2018)

Bartnik, E. (2010). Putting people in control: reforming the system of support for disabled people. In Gregg, P., & Cooks, G. (eds.). *Liberation welfare*. London: Demos. Available at: www.demos.co.uk/files/Liberation_welfare_-_web_final.pdf?1271779162 (downloaded 05.11.2018)

Bickerdike, L., Booth, A., Wilson, P. M., Farley, K., & Wright, K. (2017). Social prescribing: less rhetoric and more reality. A systematic review of the evidence. *BMJ Open, 7*(4), e013384.

Broad, R. (2012). Local Area Coordination: from service users to citizens. Available at: www.centreforwelfarereform.org/uploads/attachment/340/local-area-coordination.pdf (downloaded 05.11.2018)

Broad, R. (2015). *People, places, possibilities. Progress on Local Area Coordination in England and Wales*. Available at: www.centreforwelfarereform.org/uploads/attachment/463/people-places-possibilities.pdf (downloaded 05.11.2018)

Chadbourne, R. (2003). *A review of research on Local Area Coordination in Western Australia, consultant's report to the Local Area Coordination steering committee*. Perth: Edith Cowan University.

Deloites & NAPC. (2017). *The Primary Care Navigator programme for dementia: benefits of alternative working models*. Available at: http://napc.co.uk/wp-content/uploads/2017/09/PCN_Case_Study_Report.pdf (downloaded 05.11.2018)

Department of Health. (1999). *Effective care co-ordination in mental health services: modernising the Care Programme Approach*. London: Department of Health.

Department of Health. (2008). *Refocusing the Care Programme Approach: policy and positive practice guidance*. London: Department of Health.

General Practitioners at the Deep End. (2010). *Report 8, social pre-scribing*. Available at: www.gla.ac.uk/media/media_179091_en. pdf (downloaded 05.11.2018)

Goodwin, N., & Lawton-Smith, S. (2010). Integrating care for people with mental illness: the Care Programme Approach in England and its implications for long-term conditions manage-ment. *International Journal of Integrated Care, 10*, 1–10.

Goodwin, N., Sonola, L., Thiel, V., & Kodner, D. L. (2013). *Co-ordinated care for people with complex chronic conditions. Key lessons and markers for success*. Available at: www.kingsfund. org.uk/projects/co-ordinated-care-people-complex-chronic-condi tions (downloaded 05.11.2018)

Gulliford, M., Naithani, S., & Morgan, M. (2006). What is 'continuity of care'? *Journal of Health Services Research & Policy, 11*(4), 248–250.

Hannigan, B., Simpson, A., Coffey, M., Barlow, S., & Jones, A. (2018). Care coordination as imagined, care coordination as done: findings from a cross-national mental health systems study. *International Journal of Integrated Care, 18*(3), 12, 1–14.

Health & Social Care Alliance. (2018). *GP practice development*. Available at: www.alliance-scotland.org.uk/in-the-community/ national-link-programme/participating-gp-practices/#expanded (downloaded 05.11.2018)

Hill, K., Craston, M., Daff, K., & Thom, G. (2014). *Thematic report: key working and workforce development (pt 1)*. Available at: www. gov.uk/government/publications/send-pathfinder-programme-work force-development (downloaded 05.11.2018)

Kingfishers. (2015). *Social value of Local Area Coordination in Thur-rock*. Available at: www.thurrock.gov.uk/sites/default/files/assets/ documents/lac_report_2015.pdf (downloaded 05.11.2018)

LGA & NHS England. (2016). *Integrated personal commissioning: emerging framework*. Available at: www.england.nhs.uk/wp-con tent/uploads/2017/06/ipc-emerging-framework.pdf (downloaded 05.11.2018)

Mercer, S.W., Fitzpatrick, B., Grant, L., Chng, N. R., O'Donnell, C. A., Mackenzie, M., ... Wyke, S. (2017). The Glasgow 'Deep End' links worker study protocol: a quasi-experimental evaluation of a social prescribing intervention for patients with complex needs in areas of high socioeconomic deprivation. *Journal of Comorbidity*, 7(1), 1–10.

National Coalition on Care Coordination. (2011). Implementing Care Coordination in the Patient Protection and Affordable Care Act [online]. *Policy Brief*. Available at: www.rush.edu/sites/default/files/Implementing%20Care%20Coordination%20in%20the%20Patient%20Protection%20and%20Affordable%20Care%20Act.pdf (downloaded on 05.11.2018)

NHS England. (2016a). *Social prescribing at a glance. A scoping report of activity for the North West*. Available at: www.hee.nhs.uk/sites/default/files/documents/Social%20Prescribing%20at%20a%20glance.pdf (downloaded 05.11.2018)

NHS England. (2016b). *General practice forward view*. Available at: www.england.nhs.uk/gp/gpfv/(downloaded 05.11.2018)

NHS England. (2018). *IPC areas*. Available at: www.england.nhs.uk/ipc/ipc-areas/ (downloaded 05.11.2018)

Øvretveit, J. (2011). *Does clinical coordination improve quality and save money? A summary of a review of the evidence*. London: Health Foundation.

Polley, M. J., & Pilkington, K. (2017). *A review of the evidence assessing impact of social prescribing on healthcare demand and cost implications*. Available at: https://westminsterresearch.westminster.ac.uk/item/q1455/a-review-of-the-evidence-assessing-impact-of-social-prescribing-on-healthcare-demand-and-cost-implications (downloaded 05.11.2018)

Primary Care Hub. (2018). *Social prescribing in Wales*. Available at: www.primarycareone.wales.nhs.uk/sitesplus/documents/1191/Social%20Prescribing%20Final%20Report%20v9%202018.pdf (downloaded 05.11.2018)

SCIE. (2014). *Examples from emerging practice for integrating personal budgets for people with mental health problems*. Available at: www.scie.org.uk/publications/guides/55-integrating-personal-budgets-for-people-with-mental-health-problems/examples-from-emerging-practice.asp#example1 (downloaded 05.11.2018)

Sheaff, R., Halliday, J., Ovretveit, J., Byng, R., Exworthy, M., Peckham, S., & Asthana, S. (2015). Integration and continuity of primary care: polyclinics and alternatives – a patient-centred analysis of how organisation constrains care co-ordination. *Health Services and Delivery Research Volume*, *3*(35), 1–141.

Snitch, T. (2013). *Local Area Coordination: first four months evaluation report*. Thurrock: Thurrock Council.

Stalker, K., Malloch, M., Barry, M., & Watson, J. (2007). *Evaluation of the implementation of Local Area Coordination in Scotland*. Edinburgh: Scottish Executive.

Torjesen, I. (2016). Social prescribing could help alleviate pressure on GPs. *BMJ*, *352*, i1436.

University of York. (2015). *Evidence to inform the commissioning of social prescribing*. Available at: www.york.ac.uk/media/crd/Ev%20briefing_social_prescribing.pdf (downloaded 05.11.2018)

Vincent, A. (2010). Local Area Coordination: an exploration of practice developments in Western Australia and Northern Ireland. *Practice: Social Work in Action*, *22*(4), 203–216.

Welsh Assembly Government. (2003). *Mental health policy guidance: the Care Programme Approach for mental health service users*. Cardiff: Welsh Assembly Government.

Welsh Assembly Government. (2012). *Code of Practice to Parts 2 and 3 of the Mental Health (Wales) Measure 2010*. Available at: www.rcpsych.ac.uk/pdf/Code%20of%20Practice.pdf   (downloaded 05.11.2018)

Welsh Assembly Government. (2015). *The Duty to Review Final Report Post-Legislative Assessment of the Mental Health (Wales) Measure 2010*. Available at: www.wales.nhs.uk/sitesplus/documents/862/Item18a.MeasureDutyToReviewFinal%20Dec15%282%29.pdf (downloaded 05.11.2018)

Welsh Assembly Government. (2016). *Research to support the Duty to Review the Mental Health (Wales) Measure 2010: qualitative evidence on the views of service users, carers and practitioners.*

Available at: https://gov.wales/statistics-and-research/research-support-duty-review-mental-health-measure-2010/?lang=en (downloaded 05.11.2018)

WHO. (2018). *Continuity and coordination of care: a practice brief to support implementation of the WHO framework on integrated people-centred health services*. Available at: http://apps.who.int/iris/bitstream/handle/10665/274628/9789241514033-eng.pdf?ua=1 (downloaded 05.11.2018)

6 Integrating through professionals

A significant element of people's experience of integrated care is based on their interactions with the various professionals who provide their support. The nature of these relationships will indicate to people if there is good or poor coordination between services. A social worker who seems unaware of the involvement of a child psychologist, a general practitioner who does not understand the role of a housing support worker, and a teacher who is confused by the transition process to adult care will suggest to people that there is not sufficient communication and linkage across their services. The evidence set out in Chapter 4 highlights that there may be multiple causes of professional behaviour that fails to support integrated care. Whilst the person and their family may be understanding of these wider failings and pressures, they are likely to also feel frustration with the professionals concerned. This can be extremely demoralising for all concerned and result in a distancing in the relationship. It is also the case that professionals can sometimes ensure an integrated experience despite the messiness within the systems that lie behind them. This will often require considerable personal dedication and even the most dedicated and able professional must have their limits.

Supporting professional practice to become more collaborative is therefore a common focus of integrated care strategies. Evidence reflects that even with a supportive context not all professionals work as collaboratively as is necessary for people to experience integrated care. Indeed, research suggests that this may commonly be the case. There are many potential factors behind such failings in practice. Professionals do not always recognise that what they are doing (or not doing) is leading to fragmented care. This may be due to a lack of data that would highlight such deficits and how their practice has contributed. They may realise that the care is not ideal but find it easier to identify the flaws of others, or the failings of the system, before recognising the contribution of their own practice. Even when there is a strong local case for change and a well-designed approach to achieving better integrated care there can still be professional resistance. This may be due to anxiety about what they will be expected to do in the new arrangements or an unwillingness to give up practices with which they feel comfortable. Concerns can also arise relating to a loss of autonomy if professionals are to become more transparent and therefore accountable in their work to an inter-professional team. All these factors contribute to how motivated a professional will be to alter their practice and embrace new opportunities. In this chapter we will consider three approaches which seek to facilitate changes in professional behaviour. These reflect the Rainbow Model of Integrated Care in that practice is not only determined by the skills and knowledge of the professionals but also the physical and service environment in which they are expected to work.

> Imagine that you meet a professional from another country who is unfamiliar with the profession of social work. How would you describe social work to them, including its role, responsibilities and registration requirements? What would you say are its strengths are as a profession, and its principle contributions to more integrated care?

Training and development

Professionals need to be competent to provide more integrated care. Competency is often considered to have three elements – knowledge, skills and values. The WHO competency framework was developed to support the implementation of the global strategy. It is based on a literature review and workshops with experts on integrated care (Langins & Borgermans 2015). These sought to identify and then prioritise the competences which would best support the achievement of comprehensiveness, coordination and people-centredness (Table 6.1). The Interprofessional Education Collaborative brought together several professional educational organisations in the USA in 2009. It developed competences for collaboration to be adopted by professional bodies and taught by educational institutions (IPEC 2016). These were then updated in 2016. Training and development to support professionals to be able to demonstrate these competences has been delivered across all of their careers stages – pre-qualification in undergraduate degrees, post-graduate in masters and specialist professional qualifications, and through continuing professional development (Table 6.2).

Table 6.1 Competency clusters for integrated care (based on Langins & Borgermans 2015)

Competency cluster	Description
Patient advocacy	Ability to promote patients' entitlement to ensure the best quality of care and empowering patients to become active participants in their health
Effective communication	Ability to quickly establish rapport with patients and their family members in an empathetic and sensitive manner incorporating the patients' perceived and declared culture
Team work	Ability to function effectively as a member of an inter-professional team that includes providers, patients and family members in a way that reflects an understanding of team dynamics and group/team processes in building productive working relationships and is focused on health outcomes
People-centred care	Ability to create conditions for providing coordinated/integrated services centred on the patients and their families' needs, values and preferences along a continuum of care and over the life-course
Continuous learning	Ability to demonstrate reflective practice, based on the best available evidence and to assess and continually improve the services delivered as an individual provider and as a member of an inter-professional team

Table 6.2 Competences for inter-professional collaborative practice (based on IPEC 2016)

Domain	Detail
Values and ethics	Work with individuals of other professions to maintain a climate of mutual respect and shared values
Roles and responsibilities	Use the knowledge of one's own role and those of other professions to appropriately assess and address the health care needs of patients and to promote and advance the health of populations
Interprofessional communication	Communicate with patients, families, communities and professionals in health and other fields in a responsive and responsible manner that supports a team approach to the promotion and maintenance of health and the prevention and treatment of disease
Teams and teamwork	Apply relationship-building values and the principles of team dynamics to perform effectively in different team roles to plan, deliver and evaluate patient/population-centred care and population health programmes and policies that are safe, timely, efficient, effective and equitable

How could training and development provide more integrated care?

Undergraduate training has traditionally been carried out in a uni-professional setting in which students learn only with others doing the same course from people who are already qualified in that profession. This can mean that at graduation they have limited knowledge of the roles and expertise of other professions. Students are socialised into the values and norms of their profession which can include misleading assumptions and negative stereotypes about the work of other disciplines. Training could provide the correct information for students and those who are already qualified and in practice. Learning with and from other disciplines, through inter-professional education, could provide a powerful opportunity for sharing of insights and to challenge unhelpful perceptions.

The Leicester Model

The Leicester Model of Inter-professional Education has been deployed with undergraduate and postgraduate students. Professions involved include social workers, doctors and nurses. Students work in inter-professional learner groups of four. Individual patients are interviewed by a learner group to understand their situation, find out their personal priorities and reflect on how their health and social issues contribute to their overall health and well-being. This includes asking about experience of and relationship with health and care services. Up to four agencies currently involved with each person are interviewed. This provides a comparison with the views of the individual regarding what professionals see as the strengths and weaknesses of the support package. Students consider what they have learnt to identify the most important issues that have been raised and present these back to the current services who are involved. Facilitation is provided by academic tutors from different disciplines.

The model was initially used within primary care but has subsequently been adapted for mental health and acute hospital settings. It has also been used to support learners to gain insights specifically regarding the lives of people with a disability. Working with a local organisation led by people with a disability, students meet individuals across the age range with a variety of physical, sensory and/or learning disability. This disability specific programme initially began with medical students but was then extended to social work students. Moving from a uni-professional to inter-professional approach required practical changes to timetabling and handbooks, and structured reflective time for the academic tutors to ensure that they understood how to work inter-professionally.

Evaluation of the various iterations of the programme reveal that students from social work and medicine both saw the process as enjoyable and educational. Learning was focused around gaining a better understanding of the day-to-day lives of people with a disability and a greater awareness of the role and contribution of different professionals. Challenges included a sense from social work students that there was a dominance of health perspectives due to the community hospital setting, and it was thought that more learning would have been gained with a greater range of professions (Anderson et al. 2016). The process has also brought practical issues to the attention of the current professionals (Anderson & Thorpe 2014). This includes functioning of their care teams, gaps where people were not receiving the care that was thought, and waste through duplication of processes such as assessment (Lennox & Anderson 2012). The professionals saw student groups as bringing a fresh pair of eyes that suggested connections with new community networks. Patients reported that they enjoyed participating and that students taking the time to find out about their experiences boosted their morale. Students were also helpful in sorting out practical issues such as welfare rights and referral for adaptation.

Sliding doors

Ageism means that professionals may limit their expectations of the life that an older person can expect to lead and their ability to contribute to decisions about their care. This can result in value clashes when professions collaborate, and older people not being given the opportunity to shape their care plan. This led to NHS Education for Scotland, the Scottish Social Services Council and a learning and development consultancy developing an interactive and inter-professional learning resource. Sliding Doors aims to support health and social care staff to recognise the rights of older people, see them as a community asset rather than a burden, and to work with older people towards enjoying a full life. The name comes from the film of the same title in which two possible futures for a woman are decided by her ability to enter a train carriage before the doors slide shut. In one, she catches a tube train, meets someone and finds love and fulfilment. In the other, she misses the train and her life continues as a struggle.

Catching the train is a turning point for the possible futures that she will follow.

The Sliding Doors workshops include the following elements:

- To help connect with the challenges faced by the older people in the drama, it begins by participants considering what 'a good life' means to them.
- Actors portraying 'Maggie', an older woman with dementia, diabetes and depression and 'Iain', her husband then interrupt the participants' discussions. Led by a 'director' the characters play out what a 'good life' means for them. Participants identify what the main elements are and work in groups to discuss what they would need to do as professionals to support Maggie and Iain to have such lives.
- The drama then picks up two years later when Iain has to go into hospital for a minor operation and Maggie has become more frail. It considers two different situations which could arise from how professionals respond, and how these could affect Maggie and Iain's quality of life.
- Participants reflect on this 'turning point' and what it means for their individual and collective practice. They are directly challenged by Iain and Maggie to commit to actions that will help other older people stay close to what is important for their 'good life'.

The workshops have largely been offered as continuing professional development for those working in health and social care. The resource has also been piloted with social work and nursing students. An evaluation of its use in the University of Dundee reported that the students could see the benefits of engaging in this experience with those from another profession (Dingwall et al. 2017). However, it also revealed that the students had strong stereotypes which were not challenged through the training and if anything reinforced their views. For example, social work students saw the nurses as not being holistic or person centred, and the nurses thought that the social work students were not aware of the level of care that such a couple may need.

Improving collaboration between general practice and social work

Social workers and general practitioners are the points of entry and lead co-ordinators of publicly funded health and social care services. The extent to which they can collaborate is therefore an important element of people experiencing integrated care. Despite the centrality of this relationship, there has been surprisingly little research and what is available suggests that it has often been difficult. An action research project therefore sought to learn more about the relationship and develop work-based learning resources to improve their ability to collaborate. It was based around five general practices and their linked social work teams. These were selected to ensure that they reflected localities with different socio-demographic profiles. Focus groups were undertaken within each general practice and their link social work team to understand their experience of collaboration. Topics included:

- their current understanding of the other service's roles and professions,
- the aspects of the other service that they would find most helpful to know more about,
- what they found frustrating or helpful in working with the other service,
- experiences of previous CPD which sought to promote more collaborative working,
- parameters which they would put around such training (e.g. timing, length) and any suggestions that they would have regarding content.

The research highlighted many issues regarding the relationship between social work teams and general practice (Mangan et al. 2015). This included a lack of understanding by general practices as to the qualifications and professional status of social workers, uncertainty by social workers of the role of practice managers, and considerable difficulties in communication and negotiation.

Participants welcomed the opportunity to learn with and about the other service, but were clear that due to other pressures such a development session could last no longer than four hours, and ideally be capable of division into two session of two hours to provide maximum flexibility. The subsequent CPD programme was structured into four activities:

Activity 1: Sharing impressions

As a whole group, participants consider quotes from the research that highlight themes that were identified about collaboration between general practice and social work teams. The discussion begins to expose the common stereotypes and misperceptions held between professions.

Activity 2: Sharing knowledge

Participants work in their service groups and attempt to answer questions about the remit, organisation and professions based in the other service. For example, the general practice is asked about the professional registration requirements of a social worker. The groups then come together, and their answers are shared. The correct response is provided for discussion by the other service (e.g. the social work team will clarify the qualification and registration process for social workers).

Activity 3: Sharing roles, values and conflict

In small groups with a mixture of professions, participants consider a case scenario involving a vulnerable adult and their family carer. They discuss which professions could contribute to the person's support, potential clashes in professional values and how they would assess risk.

Activity 4: Sharing future ways of working

The final session asks participants to reflect on their learning, and then identify and commit to effective ways of working with each other.

The CPD sessions were piloted with the general practices and social work teams who had participated in the research. These sessions ended with a group discussion on 'what was helpful' and 'what could be improved', and participants completed an individual on-line survey. This suggested that the experience had been positive, however a six-month follow up was not able to engage participants to assess any impacts on their collaboration.

Discussion

There has been interest in the potential of learning and development, and in particular that which involves inter-professional approaches, for many years. The Centre for the Advancement of Interprofessional Education (CAIPE) was launched in 1987 to promote health and wellbeing and improve health and social care. It has developed clear definitions of IPE ('when two or more professions learn with, from and about each other to improve collaboration and the quality of care'), provided quality principles to guide the development of IPE and produced considerable resources to support its implementation. Many IPE programmes draw on similar theories of learning which results in them including common elements – team-based working, a focus on a real person and/or work-based issue, reflection during and after experiential elements, social interaction (including the potential for constructive challenge) and direct involvement of people or families.

A systematic review found that learners responded well to IPE, their attitudes/perceptions of one another improved and they gained knowledge and skills necessary for collaborative practice (Reeves et al. 2016). Fourteen (out of 46) studies reported changes to organisational practice and of these, 11 reported positive outcomes, and 11 (out of 46) studies reported changes to patient/service user outcomes, and of these nine reported positive outcomes. Successful implementation and sustainability of IPE innovations is related to the nature of the programmes, and the organisational and policy environments in which they are located. Implementation challenges within universities include the logistical complexities of different scheduling between programmes, courses already experiencing full timetables, tutors not always being confident of teaching other disciplines and disparities in student numbers between professions (Clouder et al. 2017). Logistics, capacity and resources are also practical issues for CPD for qualified professionals. Those already in work may not see such learning as a priority for their time and can be unwilling to address their stereotypes about the abilities of other professionals.

Teams

Most people who work in health and social care will be employed as part of a team. This may be made up of those from the same profession, such as a home care or nursing team, or those from different professions who are employed by the same organisation to support a similar population. For example, social work teams within a local authority could include social workers, social work assistants and administrative staff. Beyond the frontline of delivery, those undertaking other functions in an organisation will belong to teams within finance, human resources or legal departments. Such teams will often be the work group with which people most identify and see as their 'home' within an organisational. It will provide an immediate community where people expect to receive peer support, informal guidance and engage with management. Alongside their home team, most professionals will be part of other teams. These may be organised on a time limited basis in connection with the development of an identified project, or may be long-standing entities with responsibility for overseeing policy and practice within a particular aspect of the organisation or service. For example, it will be common for managers of children's social work teams within a local authority to meet on a monthly basis as part of a service management team, and for those who work with a specialist role such as mental health officers to gather regularly to discuss this aspect of their work.

Whilst each team has its unique context, role and set of individuals, many years of academic study of teams in organisations, sports and the military have identified common aspects for success (see Figure 6.1). First, a team needs a clear purpose

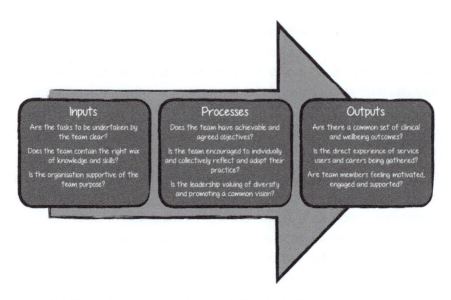

Figure 6.1 Elements of successful teams (Miller et al. 2016)

and a connected process for how its performance against this purpose will be understood. It needs sufficient capacity and diversity of expertise to undertake its allocated tasks and roles. Teams cannot though include too many members as it becomes difficult for the individuals concerned to become familiar and trusting of each other. Linked to this, it must be clear as to who is a member of the team. This can be a problem when professionals rotate through services as part of their career development, or when there is a high staff turnover or use of agency staff. Teams require pro-active leadership to ensure that they are focused and have sufficient opportunity to openly discuss relevant aspects of their work. This is commonly provided through an identified 'team leader', but can also be through more communal approaches in which team members share responsibility for co-ordination and facilitation. Finally, teams must reflect periodically on how they are performing. This should include looking at their impact and the dynamics within the team regarding decision making and managing of conflict.

How could teams provide more integrated care?

Teams bring together individuals with different skills and backgrounds around a common purpose. Certain populations will draw upon a common range of professionals and sectors to respond to their social, health and other challenges. Grouping these professionals into a team could encourage them to work together and become familiar with their respective strengths and abilities. A single team could also provide a common access point through which people can access their support.

Mental health home treatment teams

People who suffer from a serious mental illness can be subject to periods in which their difficulties become acute. During these periods they may not be able to manage through their existing informal and formal support. An intense intervention may therefore be required for a short time to enable them to stay safe and avoid, if possible, the disruption and distress connected with an admission to hospital. Crisis resolution home treatment teams are a common approach to providing such support. There was a mandate for these to be developed across England and Wales but in Scotland they were seen by government as one of the approaches that could be taken by local areas to reduce the number of people being admitted or readmitted into hospital.

A review of crisis services in Scotland in 2011 reported that three main approaches had been taken. In one of these, crisis support was undertaken by staff within the mental health services rather than as a discrete function (Williamson & Marshall 2011). In the other two, specific teams had been developed to reduce hospital admissions and to enable people to be discharged in a timely manner:

1. Separate/stand alone – a separate dedicated team included all of the main professions and connected support. Mental health

nurses were the main team member along with psychiatry, social work, psychology and occupational therapy.

2. Partially integrated – a separate dedicated team included mental health nurses and possibly a limited number of other professions but other inputs such as psychiatry and social work were drawn from generic mental health or other teams.

Introduction of a discrete team often resulted in tension with the existing inpatient and community teams. This was due to a lack of clarity regarding how the roles would connect and concerns that the capacity of the existing services would be reduced. This was in part because the team was often funded through anticipated closure of hospital beds. Such concerns were lessened if there was engagement of stakeholders in advance of implementation to explain the purpose of the team and discuss how it linked with other services. This was most effective if there was a clinical champion to promote its development and unambiguous support from senior management.

The data available suggested that the teams had made a substantial contribution to reducing the level of hospital admission and enabling more care in the community as one element of local service redesign. There were low response rates but the available feedback from people and their families was largely positive. The review concluded that it was not possible to assess which of the approaches to home treatment teams was the most effective as this was determined by a range of local factors. For stand-alone teams it was estimated that a staff group of 14–20 was required, and that it was vital for them to be multi-professional. Clarity regarding the main focus of the team being to reduce hospital admission was important to help team members prioritise their work and for other services to understand when they could draw on this support. Teams provided an opportunity for senior nurses to have greater clinical autonomy and responsibility than they would experience in a hospital setting. This was seen as positive but could require developmental opportunities and support for the nurses concerned.

Integrated primary care teams

Life expectancy is significantly lower in central Manchester than the national average of England due to high levels of deprivation and increasing prevalence of people living with multiple conditions. In the mid-2010s older people in the city had 40 per cent higher hospital admissions and 18 per cent longer bed stays than the average local authority. To respond to these challenges the health and social care commissioners and NHS providers developed an ambitious integrated care programme. This included the development of inter-professional teams around general practice.

The vision for the Practice Integrated Care Teams (PICT) was to support people who were at risk of being unable to maintain healthy and independent lives due to complex social issues and health conditions. The teams' objectives were for people to feel more confident and in control of their lives, to be seen as a whole despite the complexity of their needs, and to avoid deterioration and crisis through better planning (Beacon 2015). The core teams included general practitioners, social workers, practice nurses and community health practitioners such as district nursing and case managers. A combination of a predictive model risk stratification tool and professional judgement was used to identify people who could be at high risk and might benefit from the approach. If patients were willing to participate then they were allocated a key worker who helped people to develop personal care plans which were accessible to all team members as an electronic integrated care record.

PICTs met monthly to ensure they had opportunity to share learning and seek advice from colleagues regarding the care of people for whom they were key workers. A multi-professional group that included representatives from social work, community nursing, general practice and other professions led the initial design. The group maintained its involvement to constructively challenge and further improve the work of PICTs. Achieving the core principles required the professionals to collaborate more closely with each other and to follow a more person-centred and outcomes-orientated approach. This element of practice was challenging for some team members.

An action research evaluation was undertaken (Beacon 2015). This suggested that there had been reductions by people involved with the teams in their use of secondary care. This was challenged though by a subsequent research project which found that there had been no reduction in use of hospitals by people with more complex needs (Stokes et al. 2016). Interviews with patients and carers found they were positive about the information and support that they had received from the teams and the level of collaboration between the professionals. Professionals reported that they were working better together as the teams became established, with greater contributions from the range of disciplines. Reflecting on the development process, the lead manager identified areas that could have been more effective. This includes the involvement of patients and carers and the engagement of the voluntary and community sector. She highlighted the resistance that was encountered from some professionals to a more multidisciplinary and person-centred model. This was thought to be due to their perception that their previous role was under threat, anxiety about taking on new responsibilities and a lack of belief that the programme would be successful.

Youth offending teams

There were growing public concerns in England and Wales in the 1980s over a perceived increase in anti-social behaviour of children and young people. A lack of collective ownership by the various agencies was thought to be contributing to the worsening situation. The Crime and Disorder Act 1998 sought to legislate for a more integrated approach. It required for Youth Offending Teams to be established by all local authorities. These would be multi-agency and include involvement from social services, probation, police, health and education. Staff would be seconded into the teams (rather than funding being transferred) so that they brought knowledge and connections to their host agency. The role of the teams included providing court reports, supervising those on community sentences and supervising children and young people who had been released from custody. The Act established the Youth Justice Board as a non-departmental public body to oversee the young justice systems in England and Wales and places a duty on statutory partners to co-operate in connection with these services. Funding for Youth Offending Teams is mainly from these partners but a third is provided by the Youth Justice Board. In Wales there is also funding through the Welsh government.

Guidance in both countries emphasises the importance of the Youth Offending Team Manager. Their primary role is to oversee and coordinate the work of team members. They must ensure that there are good operational relationships with other agencies and that the local management board has the necessary information to understand the work of the team. The board in turn should support the manager in addressing partnership issues that can be sorted out at the operational level. This strategic relationship between the local partners is a key enabler for the work of the teams.

Initially Young Offending Teams were largely run as discrete entities. This provided a multidisciplinary point of focus to work with children and young people who had not always received sufficient positive attention. It resulted at times in other agencies being too keen to withdraw once the Young Offending Team became involved. This was one of the reasons that teams are becoming more integrated with other local authority services. Other factors include a decline in the numbers of children and young people supported by teams, a commitment to providing earlier intervention before problems escalated and a need to find financial savings. Similar reasons have led to local authorities merging their youth justice services to reduce costs. Financial pressures have been caused by the general time of austerity within local authorities and the other partners as well as reductions in the central grant provided to Youth Offending Teams.

A review in 2016 (Taylor 2016) reported that much good progress had been made in providing more integrated support.

However, it also highlighted that for those children and young people left in the system 'too often the shutters come down when YOTs try to get support from social care, education, housing or health for a child who needs a coordinated response if their offending is to desist' (p7). In particular, it was reported that there was often great difficulty in accessing support from Child and Adolescent Mental Health Services due to their high access thresholds. Engagement with education was an issue with many of the young people being excluded with insufficient alternative opportunities for training and learning being provided. In relation to the practice within teams, one research project found that team members from different professional backgrounds shared a common understanding of the factors that led to people engaging in such behaviour – poverty, exclusion from education and poor parenting. There were though different beliefs within teams as to how best to respond a continuum between 'welfare' and 'justice' (Morris 2015).

Discussion

Good team working has been shown to have a positive impact within general health and social care services (Jelphs et al. 2016). For example, longitudinal research in the English NHS based on the annual staff survey has shown that if a majority of staff in a hospital report being part of a well-run team then it is likely to have lower mortality rates than those with weaker team working (West et al. 2013). There is also evidence that inter-professional teams can improve people's experience and outcomes within different areas of service. Positive outcomes in cancer services include increased rates of survival; improved patient satisfaction; and better diagnosis and/or treatment planning (Prades et al. 2015). The job satisfaction and overall wellbeing of professionals working in well-run multidisciplinary teams is also higher (Reeves et al. 2011). This in turn is connected with those professionals providing a better service to the people and families that they support (Huxley et al. 2011). The evidence for cost-effectiveness is less clear, however, with studies reporting improved, unchanged or even negative impacts due to the need for investment and team-based processes (Ke et al. 2013).

Research and practice examples such as those outlined above suggest that inter-professional teams can provide a helpful vehicle to support more integrated care but there are several important caveats. If the team does not reflect the elements of good working summarised in the introduction to this section, then it will not provide the expected benefits. Indeed, it may lead both to poorer care and a more stressful working environment. Social workers are often in the position of being the non-health worker. This can lead to them feeling isolated and their perspectives being under-valued by the rest of the team. Grouping people together in a team does not by itself address traditional differentials in power and it can lead to a heightening rather than reduction in tension (Ambrose-Miller & Ashcroft 2016). If professionals are paid and/or performance managed in relation to their own activity (rather than the work of the team) then it is easy for team members to default to working in parallel (Bentley et al. 2018). This will mean that the added value of being within a team can be lost. Investing time and where necessary external support to teams can help to ensure that team members are able to work together better. One research project regarding inter-professional teams has developed materials to improve the effectiveness of inter-professional team meetings which were discussing the goals and care plans of people with chronic disease (van Dongen et al. 2018). This is based on a series of questions with training sessions and a 'tool box' to guide good team working practice.

Co-location and joint management

An artefact of the development of separate sectors and specialisms within the UK welfare state is that many of our services are based in different physical locations. For example, education services are housed in schools, primary care services within general practices and social work within local authority buildings. There is an obvious practical logic to such arrangements. They are financially simpler (as the employing organisation will use its budgets to employee staff and maintain or lease the buildings) and they provide an environment in which professionals with a shared or connected responsibility can engage with colleagues. It does create geographical silos in which professionals from different backgrounds have little interaction with each other unless it is connection with a specific person, family or other matter. In many instances professionals may never actually physically meet someone employed in a different service as communication will be virtual. This will probably have little impact on more simple matters but can pose difficulties if the issue to be resolved is less clear or contested.

Alongside the issue of location is that of siloed management. For similar reasons of organisational coherence and logistical ease, it is common for the professionals working within different services to have separate management arrangements. The managers will be responsible for ensuring that the services adhere to organisational procedures relating to health and safety, financial management and human resources. Managers are tasked with using the allocated resources to fulfil the objectives set by its governing board or equivalent. They provide appraisals and work with staff members to develop their personal development plan to respond to current responsibilities and future career options. The manager is in many ways an embodiment of the organisation concerned and its distinct set of institutional norms and values. In relation to integrated care, they will often have a key role in deciding how flexible the service will be in responding to people who do not neatly fit into the criteria or services options, and how actively the service will seek to engage with other professions and services.

Both location and management arrangements therefore potentially contribute to people's care being more or less integrated. Co-locating services and having a single manager to oversee the various resources within a service is common within single organisations. For example, a single large hospital will contain accident and emergency, surgical wards, out-patients, diagnostic facilities and so on. Outside social work and its related fields, co-location is seen to generate creative thinking and responses to complex problems. This includes within the tech industry, with developers from companies such as Microsoft and Google clustering in geographic locations such as Seattle and Mountain View (Memon & Kinder 2017).

How could co-location and joint management provide more integrated care?

If professionals are based in the same location, then their proximity could enable them to develop a greater understanding of each other's roles and familiarity with each other as individuals. This could lead to a confidence in working with those of a different background and the development of reciprocity and trust. A single manager who oversees a service which brings together professionals from various organisations could help interpret their different procedures and policies and provide a common point of coordination and oversight.

Co-location of advice workers and general practice in Glasgow

Poverty is recognised as a major factor which can adversely affect people's health and wellbeing. For example, it can make it hard to adopt and maintain healthy behaviours such as eating and exercise and lead to increased feelings of stress and a loss of control. It has an amplifying effect on inequalities within society through preventing people being able to access employment or training activities. This contributes to chilling statistics such as the healthy life expectancy gap between most and least deprived parts of the UK being 19 years (Lawson 2018). In many cases people and families may not be aware of the all of the options that are available to them in respect of increasing their income or addressing issues such as rent arrears or unpaid loans. Improving their access to advice services can therefore help them to access relevant information and support them in advocating for their rights and entitlements.

The Deep End Advice Worker project in Glasgow was developed to improve the access of people living in Parkhead to welfare benefits and other financial support (Sinclair 2017). This is one of the 20 per cent most deprived areas in Scotland and some neighbourhoods are classed as the 5 per cent most deprived in the country. Two general practices participated which support approximately 3,200 and 4,700 patients. The projects were overseen by an advisory group that included general practitioners, health improvement workers and a local money advice project. They met regularly to consider activity, impacts such as financial gain and debt reduction and how the arrangements could be more effective. The project became part of a wider programme funded by the Joseph Rowntree Foundation that was looking to promote better collaboration between public and third sectors. This enabled the support of a programme manager to help with gathering learning and improving the processes.

An advice worker is based in each practice for half a day per week. They have an expert knowledge of options for support with good working relationships with local organisations that provide direct and indirect support. People can be referred to the advice worker by their general practitioner or by another member of staff with whom they have raised a relevant issue. This includes reception staff. People are referred via an email to keep the process to a minimum and the worker will undertake an initial telephone triage. If they require an appointment then this is held on the first occasion in a consultation room within the practice.

The evaluation of the service found that over an 18-month period 165 people engaged with the service (65 per cent of people who were initially referred). Referral rates within these practices were much higher than those of non co-located advice services. The people concerned were predominantly those experiencing significant poverty and most had mental health issues and/or a long-term illness. The service was able to generate almost £850,000 for the individuals concerned and managed over £150,000 worth of debt.

Alongside the co-location, the other aspects of the arrangements that were seen as important were that the advice worker mirrored the other professionals in relation to their attire and their working practices. For example, they used the same system to call people into their consultation room. This meant that people accessing the advice were not distinguished from patients but could access the service discretely. With the person's consent, the advice worker could access their medical notes. This enabled them to gather relevant details from their histories, provide an update for the general practitioners and co-produce required medical reports. Advice workers also sought to create good working relationships with other practice staff through sharing social interactions. All these activities were seen as playing a significant role in helping the advice workers become 'embedded' and not just 'located' in the practices.

Integrated support service for children and young people with a disability

Children with a disability and their families can require support from a range of education, health and social care professionals and services throughout their life course. Dependent on when their disabilities are recognised, this can begin before they attend school and carry on into adult life. This means that they can experience several transitions as they progress in age. For example, between pre-school, primary school, secondary school and college, between children's and adult social work services and from paediatric to adult health care services. Such transitions can be highly disruptive as the individual and their family have to leave behind professionals and services with whom they have an existing relationship. Furthermore, the service that they will be accessing may have a different model, criteria and funding arrangement. The problems that many people experience in the transition to adult services seem to have been long standing despite numerous strategies over the decades to improve this process.

The Sandwell Integrated Support Service was developed to provide more integrated care for children and young people with disabilities and their families. It incorporated services from education, social work, health, youth services and careers guidance. These involved professionals including teachers of people with a sensory impairment, psychologists, learning disability nurses, social workers and counsellors. These included those who worked with adults as well as children so that the service could act as a bridge as people left school and transitioned into adult life and the associated supports. The staff remained employed by their host organisations and were seconded in to the service.

To encourage more collaborative working between the various teams and professionals, all the members of the service were based in a refurbished building. This provided office accommodation, consultation and meeting rooms, and housed the early years development centre. There was a single service manager appointed to oversee the service and to provide line management support for all the managers of the individual teams. A common access point and single referral pathway was introduced which included a weekly multidisciplinary discussion of people who had been referred and the outcome of their initial assessment. The service was overseen by a multi-agency steering group involving the agencies which had contributed resources to the service.

Moving into the building required the teams concerned to leave existing arrangements in which they have been based with people from a similar profession and/or employed by a similar organisation. This resulted in some disciplines reporting that they felt isolated from similar professional colleagues. Rather than mingle together, the professional teams chose to sit in different offices or discrete areas of the large shared office space and continued to hold individual team meetings. Due to the large number of people housed in the building and an aspiration to reduce car usage there was often insufficient parking spaces available on site at peak times of the day. This resulted in considerable frustration and tension if someone's car was blocked by another worker with some examples of this being used to stereotype the behaviour of other teams.

This meant that the service was in danger of continuing as a set of parallel teams rather than as an integrated whole. The management team therefore organised periodic development days in which the service would engage in inter-professional discussions about their work and reflect on the needs of case study children and young people. The service organised family days which would provide a range of activities for young people and their families. There were highly rated by families and staff, as it provided an opportunity to work across their usual professional boundaries. To understand the impacts of the service a university was asked to undertake an independent evaluation of the outcomes and implementation. This gathered and compared the perspectives of staff and families through surveys and interviews (Dickinson et al. 2009). The staff believed that the service had strong aims and objectives but these were largely connected with the process of integration. They struggled to articulate what these outcomes would look like for children and their families. Families reported that the service had been slow to become operational but that over time it was working better. They did not identify practical barriers such as parking which staff thought would be a major problem for their access. They did though highlight that many of the services that they needed were not included in the service or based on the site, meaning that there had been little improvement in their access or the coordination of this support.

Discussion

Bringing together professionals to work from the same physical locality would seem a practical solution to the common lack of knowledge of and interaction between them. This has been described as a theory of 'spacial proximity' which predicts that geographic closeness will reduce the effort required to communicate and enable connection by those from different back-grounds but with similar communication styles. The examples above suggest that co-location can be a facilitator of collaboration but that this is far from guaranteed. This reflects the findings from research. For example, one study in Wales explored two integrated health and social care teams for children with a disability in the same Health Board area which were co-located to improve their joint working (Kaehne & Catherall 2012). Positives reported by professionals included more holistic discussion of the individuals and their families and improved communication. Weaknesses included co-location resulting in distance from other relevant services which were not based in the building and that the disruption of the move did not ultimately lead to improvements in working practices. A survey of professionals suggested that the majority (86 per cent) thought that the change had made their work harder not easier, and around half were sceptical that there had been improvements in the care for individuals and their families. Similarly, a study in Denmark found that a lack of vision about what the new collaborations would be and a lack of shared commitment from the professionals concerned meant that there was little positive impact from moving them into the same building (Scheele & Vrangbæk 2016).

Operational managers are recognised in all industries as making a key contribution to the climate and working culture of a service. These help to set the foundations on which the professionals will be supported, inspired and if necessary challenged to deliver services of a high quality. Managers are though only part of the management system within an organisation. Therefore, whilst they are influential with their teams this is situated in a wider context of resource prioritisation, performance management and incentive systems (Atkinson et al. 2007). Furthermore, the managers themselves will vary as to their understanding of how integrated care can be supported and will have their own style of management. This may be more familiar to those from a similar professional background within the integrated service and less comfortable to those from different backgrounds. For example, there are differing expectations as to the role of managers regarding oversight of their professional decision making and who would provide professional supervision. Research has shown that style of management is a significant factor in job satisfaction, quality of care, teamwork and integration of team professionals within mental health services (Huxley et al. 2011). Despite the important contribution of managers, it is therefore surprising how few development opportunities exist to support managers to gain the necessary insights and skills to lead integrated services.

Consider a social work or inter-professional team in which you have worked or undertaken a placement. Using the model in Figure 6.1, represent the inputs, processes and outcomes for the team. Which were clear when you were part of the team? For the other aspects, would there have been differences of opinion between team members?

Further resources

Centre for the Advancement of Interprofessional Education
www.caipe.org

The Centre for the Advancement of Interprofessional Education (CAIPE) is a membership organisation and UK-based charity that promotes health and wellbeing and works to improve the health and social care of the public by advancing interprofessional education.

European Forum for Primary Care www.euprimarycare.org

A network of health and care professionals across Europe who are interested in better collaboration around people and communities.

Journal of Interprofessional Care www.tandfonline.com/toc/ijic20/current

This journal aims to disseminate research and new developments in the field of inter-professional education and practice.

Interprofessional Education Collaborative www.
ipecollaborative.org

A USA based collaborative to promote and encourage constituent efforts to advance substantive inter-professional learning experiences to help prepare future health and care professionals for enhanced team-based care and improved population health outcomes.

References

Ambrose-Miller, W., & Ashcroft, R. (2016). Challenges faced by social workers as members of interprofessional collaborative health care teams. *Health & Social Work, 41*(2), 101–109.

Anderson, E., Smith, R., & Hammick, M. (2016). Evaluating an inter-professional education curriculum: a theory-informed approach. *Medical Teacher, 38*(4), 385–394.

Anderson, E., & Thorpe, L. (2014). Students improve patient care and prepare for professional practice: an interprofessional community-based study. *Medical Teacher, 36*(6), 495–504.

Atkinson, M., Jones, M., & Lamont, E. (2007). *Multi-agency working and its implications for practice*. Reading: CfBT Education Trust. Available at: www.nfer.ac.uk/multi-agency-working-and-its-implications-for-practice-a-review-of-the-literature (downloaded 05.11.2018)

Beacon, A. (2015). Practice-integrated care teams – learning for a better future. *Journal of Integrated Care, 23*(2), 74–87.

Bentley, M., Freeman, T., Baum, F., & Javanparast, S. (2018). Inter-professional teamwork in comprehensive primary healthcare services: findings from a mixed methods study. *Journal of Interprofessional Care, 32*(3), 274–283.

Clouder, L., Daly, G., Adefila, A., Jackson, A., Furlong, J., & Bluteau, P. (2017). *An investigation to understand and evaluate the best ways to educate for and promote integrated working across the health and care sectors*. Available at: https://cele. coventry.ac.uk/celewordpress/wp-content/uploads/2012/05/ integrated_working_report23rdjune2017.pdf (downloaded 05.11. 2018)

Dickinson, H., Glasby, J., Miller, R., & McArthy, L. (2009). Whose outcomes are they anyway? Report of the pilot evaluation of a joint service. *Journal of Integrated Care*, *17*(1), 37–44.

Dingwall, L., Fenton, J., Kelly, T. B., & Lee, J. (2017). Sliding Doors: did drama-based inter-professional education improve the tensions round person-centred nursing and social care delivery for people with dementia: a mixed method exploratory study. *Nurse Education Today*, *51*, 1–7.

Huxley, P., Evans, S., Baker, C. White, J., Philpin, S., Onyett, S., & Gould, N. (2011). Integration of social care staff within community mental health teams. Final report. London: National Institute for Health Research (NIHR) Service Delivery and Organisation Programme.

IPEC. (2016). *Core Competencies for Interprofessional Collaborative Practice*. Available at: https://hsc.unm.edu/ipe/resources/ index.html (downloaded 05.11.2018)

Jelphs, K., Dickinson, H., & Miller, R. (2016). *Working in teams*. Bristol: Policy Press.

Kaehne, A., & Catherall, C. (2012). Co-located health and social care services in Wales: what are the benefits to professionals? *International Journal of Healthcare Management*, *5*(3), 164–172.

Ke, K. M., Blazeby, J. M., Strong, S., Carroll, F. E., Ness, A. R., & Hollingworth, W. (2013). Are multidisciplinary teams in secondary care cost-effective? A systematic review of the literature. *Cost Effectiveness and Resource Allocation*, *11*(7), 1–13.

Langins, M., & Borgermans, L. (2015). *Strengthening a competent health workforce for the provision of coordinated/integrated health services*. Available at: www.euro.who.int/__data/assets/pdf_file/ 0010/288253/HWF-Competencies-Paper-160915-final.pdf (downloaded 05.11.2018)

Lawson, S. (2018). *Infographic: poverty and health*. Available at: www.health.org.uk/blog/infographic-poverty-and-health (downloaded 05.11.2018)

Lennox, A., & Anderson, E. (2012). Delivering improvements in patient care: the application of the Leicester Model of Interprofessional Education. *Quality in Primary Care*, *20*(3), 219–226.

Mangan, C., Miller, R., & Ward, C. (2015). Knowing me, knowing you: inter-professional working between general practice and social care. *Journal of Integrated Care*, *23*(2), 62–73.

Memon, A., & Kinder, T. (2017). Co-location as a catalyst for service innovation: a study of Scottish health and social care. *Public Management Review*, *19*(4), 381–405.

Miller, R., Brown, H., & Mangan, C. (2016). *Integrated care in action: a practical guide for health, social care and housing support*. London: Jessica Kingsley.

Morris, R. (2015). Youth justice practice is just messy. *British Journal of Community Justice*, *13*(2), 47–58.

Prades, J., Remue, E., Van Hoof, E., & Borras, J. M. (2015). Is it worth reorganising cancer services on the basis of multidisciplinary teams (MDTs)? A systematic review of the objectives and organisation of MDTs and their impact on patient outcomes. *Health Policy*, *119*(4), 464–474.

Reeves, S., Fletcher, S., Barr, H., Birch, I., Boet, S., Davies, N., ... Kitto, S. (2016). A BEME systematic review of the effects of interprofessional education: BEME Guide No. 39. *Medical Teacher*, *38*(7), 656–668.

Reeves, S., Lewin, S., Espin, S., & Zwarenstein, M. (2011). *Interprofessional teamwork for health and social care*. Chichester: John Wiley.

Scheele, C. E., & Vrangbæk, K. (2016). Co-location as a driver for cross-sectoral collaboration with general practitioners as coordinators: the case of a Danish Municipal Health Centre. *International Journal of Integrated Care*, *16*(4), 1–11, 15.

Sinclair, J. (2017). *The Deep End Advice Worker project*. Available at: www.gcph.co.uk/publications/728_the_deep_end_advice_

worker_project_embedding_advice_in_general_practice   (downloaded 05.11.2018)

Stokes, J., Kristensen, S. R., Checkland, K., & Bower, P. (2016). Effectiveness of multidisciplinary team case management: difference-in-differences analysis. *BMJ Open*, 6(4), 1–11.

Taylor, C. (2016). *Review of the youth justice system in England and Wales*. Available at: www.gov.uk/government/publications/review-of-the-youth-justice-system (downloaded 05.11.2018)

van Dongen, J., van Bokhoven, M., Goossens, W., Daniëls, R., van der Weijden, T., & Beurskens, A. (2018). Development of a customizable programme for improving interprofessional team meetings: an action research approach. *International Journal of Integrated Care*, *18*(1), 1–14.

West, M. A., Dawson, J., Admasachew, L., & Topakas, A. (2013). *NHS staff management and health service quality*. Available at: www.gov.uk/government/uploads/system/…data/…/dh_129656.pdf (downloaded 05.11.2018)

Williamson, P., & Marshall, L. (2011). *A review of crisis resolution home treatment services in Scotland*. Available at: www.qihub.scot.nhs.uk/media/264761/crisis_resolution_home_treatment_report%20final%20november.pdf (downloaded 05.11.2018)

7 Integrating across a system

The main approach to the organising of resources within public services is by locating resources and the associated infrastructure within organisations. These vary enormously in size, complexity, resources and geographical coverage. Large health care trusts responsible for community and hospital services, independent providers who work across many regions and different parts of the UK, and micro-enterprises delivering social inclusion support to people living within a defined geographical area have very different scales and scopes. They vary considerably in their legal status and governance structures. The accountability of a democratically elected local authority is different to that within a registered charity, state school or a private business contained within an international corporation or hedge-fund. Similarly, whilst it is hoped that they will have a common interest in providing people with a good standard and level of support, their overall purpose will vary considerably. The purpose, or mission, of an organisation determines how it will judge success and will inform decisions about the prioritisation of resources. For a private business, the key indicator will be its ability to generate profit for its owners or shareholders both now and in the future. For a charity, it will be fulfilling its objectives to promote the welfare of an identified population or cultural activity. For a local authority, it will be undertaking its legal functions and promoting the interests of the area for which it is responsible. The councillors will also be keen for them and their party to win as many seats as possible at the next election!

Despite these differences there are similarities in the core responsibilities of these organisations. They need to ensure that their services meet the quality standards set by care regulators, health and safety requirements are adhered to, finances are audited to ensure probity and staff have the necessary skills to undertake their roles. Organisations have a common need to ensure that they have sufficient resources and influence to deliver their purpose. Unlike a private business, a charity does not have to generate profit. It does though need the funding required to support its beneficiaries and to generate sufficient income to break evenly financially. Ideally they will usually want to have a surplus to enable them to respond to unmet needs which are discovered. As there are never sufficient resources to meet all of these organisational interests there is therefore an element of competition for funding. This is the case within a welfare system that is not designed primarily around a market system as such. Alongside the rivalry for resources, organisations often need each other to fulfil their objectives. For example, a hospital requires the support of a local authority to discharge people with care needs. It will not want the responsibility or funding to arrange a domiciliary care package but rather needs the local authority to undertake these duties. Without the support of the assessing social work department the hospital can therefore be criticised for not fulfilling its core duties of ensuring people are cared for in the right environment and holding on to people who are ready to be discharged. The other organisation may not see this as its main priority within its duties and interests, or recognise how important its contribution is to the overall working of the system.

Organisations are therefore central to the achievement of integrated care. Most of the policies within the nations of the UK are primarily designed to shape the behaviour of organisations. This is in the hope that they will in turn influence and direct their staff and other resources to achieve this aim. In this section we consider three of the common approaches to integrated care designed around organisations, partnership boards, integrated organisations and pooled budgets.

Many of us have only limited understanding of our employing organisations. Try to answer the following questions regarding the one in which you are currently placed/working, or have most recently done so.

- What is the governing body for the organisation and what are the types of members?
- How does it involve people and families in overseeing its strategy and quality?
- What is the organisation's vision for success and how is this being measured?
- Are there values for the organisation and do these include those relating to collaboration?

Now answer the same questions for an external organisation with which you have regular contact.

Partnership boards

Organisations require a means to oversee their various activities and ensure that their resources are being deployed effectively to achieve their overall purpose. In smaller private businesses this role will generally be taken on by the owners. In larger private organisations, and ones of all sizes from the charitable and public sectors, this will be achieved through identifying a group of people with responsibility for providing overall strategic leadership and ensuring that the organisation is compliant with its legal duties. The structure and membership of a board varies dependent on the type of organisation. Local authorities in Wales are led by cabinets composed of the overall leader (who is voted as such by the Council as a whole) and up to nine other elected members selected by the leader. Charities are led by their trustees who must act in the best interests of the charities and not for personal gain. The legal responsibilities of trustees are set out by regulators such as OSCR in Scotland and the Charity Commission for England and Wales. Foundation NHS Trusts in England are led by boards comprised of executive and non-executive officers but are accountable to governors drawn from the local community, staff representatives and other stakeholders such as the local authority and universities. Whatever the arrangement in place, the relationship between this strategic group and the senior managers within the organisation will be key to its successful function. It is the managers, often known at a senior level as the 'executive', who are responsible for its day-to-day running and turning the strategy into practical reality. Changing the behaviour of organisations to deliver more integrated care will require commitment from the board and from the executive.

How could partnership boards provide more integrated care?

Organisations that are not fully aware of how their activities can better connect may collectively miss opportunities to jointly redesign and coordinate services to the benefit of people and their families. Giving organisations a shared responsibility to respond to a particular issue may encourage them to put aside their differences and work together to avoid being labelled individually and collectively as failing to meet this responsibility. A partnership vehicle such as a board can provide a forum for their connected discussions and provide a focal point for others to engage with the work.

Community Health Partnerships

Community Health Partnerships were introduced through the NHS Reform (Scotland) Act 2004 and run as committees or sub-committees of NHS boards. Community Health Partnerships were responsible for the planning and delivery of primary and community health services in their geographical areas and addressing gaps between health and social care. This included services for children and families as well as adults. They were set nine priority areas to achieve, including tackling health inequalities, supporting more people at home and taking a systematic approach to long-term conditions. The partnerships were set within a broader policy environment which was encouraging more integration between health and social care and greater flexibility for local councils and health bodies over use of their allocated resources.

The populations for which the Community Health Partnerships were responsible varied considerably (Box 7.1). In 2010 the partnership in Orkney covered 19,960 people and in Edinburgh City 477,660 people. There could be more than one partnership covering the same council areas. The statutory guidance stated that 'no one size fits all', with flexibility for local bodies to decide how best to configure their arrangement. This included a recommended but not mandated list of potential stakeholders to be included as members. Partnerships could either take a structure that included health and social care, or one that only involved health care. This could change over time. For example, NHS Greater Glasgow and Clyde and Glasgow City Council initially developed five integrated partnerships in 2005. A review in 2010 identified fundamental problems such as the lack of a clear strategy, no firm agreement on the functions and services to be delivered, and no joint financial framework. The Integrated Community Health Partnerships were subsequently dissolved as the Council and NHS were unable to agree on how best to proceed.

Box 7.1 Examples of Community Health Partnerships (Audit Scotland 2011)

East Renfrewshire

The East Renfrewshire integrated CHP committee has a clear purpose and a joint vision, strategy and outcome measures for health and social care services for the local area. Clear leadership has enabled the committee and management team to develop a partnership ethos and culture and ensure committee members are fully informed of their role, responsibilities and the needs of their local communities so that they can make informed decisions. The NHS board and council have streamlined their partnership arrangements, dissolved the Joint Future Partnership Group and designated the CHP as the thematic health and wellbeing group of the Community Planning Partnership. The CHP leads community planning in relation to health and wellbeing for the local population. Committee meetings are well attended. The NHS board and council have appointed a joint CHP director and other joint service managers. This has enabled East Renfrewshire Council to achieve recurring efficiencies of £350,000 each year. The integrated management structure has helped to improve joint planning and delivery of services. The NHS board and council have also introduced a joint performance management framework.

Western Isles

The initial role, vision and governance structure for the integrated CHP are set out in the Scheme of Establishment although these arrangements have not been fully implemented. When the integrated CHP was being set up, a number of other joint health and social care groups and partnerships were already in place and the NHS board and the council did not take the opportunity to rationalise these. As a result, the roles and purpose of the CHP committee and other partnership groups have become increasingly blurred. The CHP committee is large with 26 members, most of whom are also involved in other partnership groups. Attendance at CHP committee meetings is consistently poor. Although Western Isles CHP is intended to be an integrated structure, the NHS board and council have their own separate managers and health and social care services are managed separately. There is also a lack of capacity within the CHP management team to carry out joint planning and performance management for health and social care.

The Audit Scotland review in 2011 described considerable diversity in the role of the Community Health Partnerships. Some areas gave them planning and prioritisation of resource allocation but in others, partnerships were limited to the delivery of specific services rather than setting of overall strategy. Only one had been given delegated responsibility for social care budgets. There was a lack of clarity about how the overall funding in some areas was being deployed and often little detail about the costs of administering the partnership itself. In relation to changing the models of care, only slight progress was made in both increasing the proportion of NHS resources being spent in the community or transferred to local authorities to support social care spend. Despite some examples of good practice, the Audit Office reported that emergency admissions for older people and delayed discharges were increasing. Partnerships would need to influence the practice of GPs to achieve a more preventative model. However, the engagement was varied and in some areas the partnership was overlooked by GPs as it was seen as having little influence.

The Audit Office concluded that strengthening the Community Health Partnerships would require local and national actions. Their role, responsibilities and accountability arrangements with the local health and social systems needed to be clarified. The performance framework and connected reporting mechanisms for the contribution of partnerships to improving health and social care services required tightening. This would require formal governance processes for the organisations concerned to be amended and for a rationalisation of the multiplicity of collaborative bodies within local areas. The Audit Office recommended that national government should assist partnerships by undertaking a more general review of its expectations. The difference in national employment terms and conditions between health and social care staff was a common source of tension.

Local Safeguarding Children Boards

There is a long history of partnership boards being deployed in England and Wales to protect and promote the welfare of children and young people. Area Child Protection Committees were established in 1988 to provide a structured approach to the coordination of the work of agencies responsible for children at risk. These were led by local authorities and over time were given increasing responsibilities including overseeing child protection registers and providing training. As non-statutory bodies they were reliant on the good will of other agencies to co-operate. Various reviews suggested that many Area Child Protection Committees experienced difficulties connected with confusion over their responsibilities, insufficient leadership and tensions between their members. The Laming Inquiry highlighted that whilst many did good work, the arrangements were seen as lacking authority and not consistently providing strategic leadership – 'unwieldy, bureaucratic and [with] limited impact' (Lord Laming 2003, p1).

Area Child Protection Committees were replaced by Local Safeguarding Children Boards in England and Wales by the Children Act 2004. These were statutory bodies which were to move beyond only responding to those who need protection to pro-actively promoting the welfare of children and preventing harm occurring. Local Authorities were again required to establish the boards but there were also duties placed on specified agencies including health, probation and police. The overall remit of the boards was 'to coordinate what is done by each person or body represented on the Board for the purposes of safeguarding and promoting the welfare of children in the area of the authority; [and] to ensure the effectiveness of what is done by each such person or body for that purpose' (Children Act 2004, Sec. 14[1]). Their functions included: developing and agreeing local safeguarding policies and procedures; providing training; making assessments about the impact and effectiveness of local safeguarding arrangements; and undertaking serious case and child death reviews. The agencies involved retained the prime responsibility for performing their individual roles and tasks, with the board providing monitoring and challenge of their work. The initial guidance was that independent chairs were preferred but not mandated as such.

A number of major reviews considered the running and impact of the boards. The review of child protection services in England by Eileen Munro (2012) recommended that their annual reports be considered by the leader and chief executive of the council and by the Police and Crime Commissioner to ensure that their work was embraced at the highest level. The review in England by Lord Laming in 2009 discovered that in many local areas there was a continued reluctance by some agencies to accept their full responsibility for safeguarding children and young people. This was contrasted with other areas in which there had been a more thorough commitment to partnership working through the work of the board (see Box 7.2). Such national reviews led to new detailed guidance being issued in 2015. This confirmed the expected membership, that the partners had to provide sufficient resources for the board to operate and that there should be an independent chair.

A further review of safeguarding services in England was published in 2016 by Alan Wood (2016). This advocated for greater flexibility be given to local areas to design the arrangements which work best in their contexts. This led to the requirement for all areas to have Safeguarding Boards being removed by the Children and Social Work Act 2017. Instead local areas were given greater flexibility over their partnership arrangements. Local

---

Box 7.2 Good practice example from Laming Progress Review (2009)

In one local authority, doing the 'basics' well has enabled the Local Safeguarding Children Board (LSCB) to develop a strong and mature partnership. The LSCB benefits from a personal commitment from Executive Directors across each of the health trusts. Four health trusts (two acute, one mental health and one primary care trust have their own safeguarding boards which meet quarterly, and are led by their respective executive directors. The function of the health safeguarding boards is to co-ordinate safeguarding practice across the trusts, ensuring a 'two-way learning and improvement dialogue' with the LSCB. These arrangements also support an annual event to consider cross boundary issues, across the trusts and two local authority areas. This has led to implementation of the same protocols regardless of the local authority area where a child or family live.

---

authorities, police and health service commissioners have a duty to introduce the approach that they think will best ensure that they and other agencies would work together. To ensure transparency the partner agencies must publish how the arrangements will work and what external scrutiny of these arrangements will be put in place.

Reviews of the effectiveness of Local Safeguarding Children Boards have also been completed in Wales. This included a major review by six government bodies (Care and Social Services Inspectorate Wales, Healthcare Inspectorate Wales, Estyn, HM Inspectorate for Education and Training in Wales, HM Inspectorate of Constabulary and HM Inspectorate of Probation) in 2008 (CCISW 2011). They reported that there were improvements in the safeguarding afforded to children and young people but that the boards were not able to demonstrate how and if they were fulfilling their responsibilities. This would require clearer objectives and better analysis of relevant data against these objectives. The National Assembly review in 2010 recommended that the Welsh government needed to provide clearer direction as to the focus of boards, the expected contribution from partner agencies, and how the boards should interact with other partnership bodies (National Assembly for Wales Health, Wellbeing and Local Government Committee 2010). Subsequent to these reviews, the 22 existing boards were merged in 2012 to form six regional Safeguarding Children Boards. Their remit was updated by the Social Services and Well-Being (Wales) Act 2014 to protect children and prevent harm through 'coordinating and ensuring the effectiveness of what is done by each person or body represented on the Board' (S.135 (3)). The Act created a National Independent Safeguarding Board to support the regional boards, report on their effectiveness and make recommendations for improvement to ministers. It also provided legislative support for regions to consider having a single safeguarding board for adults and children. By 2018 this merged option had been implemented in Mid and West Wales, and North Wales.

Research regarding the working of Local Safeguarding Children Boards in Wales and England has been consistent in its findings. Boards are only as strong as the commitment and influence of their members – if there is not local senior level sign up to these responsibilities then despite the legislative requirement, boards are unlikely to make a difference. Strong chairing is a major enabler of the board's functioning. This requires independence, skills and capacity on behalf of the person appointed to this role. Chairs must help the board to prioritise their work as if they are too ambitious then this can result in little being completed. Even the strongest chairs though have limitations in their ability to influence other agencies if these partners are fundamentally not willing or able to commit. Safeguarding Boards require resources to complete their functions – this includes the administration of the regular meeting cycle, the production of annual reports and the completion of serious case and other such reviews. A thorough but serviceable performance framework is necessary to understand progress and hold the board members collectively and individually to account. Outside the board itself, there needs to be clarity within the local area of its remit and how its work should connect with other partnership bodies.

Discussion

Partnership boards are a common approach through which it is hoped that the activities of different organisations can be better aligned and coordinated. This is based on the assumption that a 'board' of senior people can shape how a set of organisations (and in particular the staff that they employ) will behave. This is similar to the thinking about organisational boards. Research and practice indicate that there is considerable variation in their ability to operate effectively which is similar to the findings for the Partnership Board examples. They must be able to respond to a common set of questions – do they have a clear and common purpose, do they work well as a team, are they able to engage the workforce for whom they are responsible and so on. Furthermore, some organisational boards have not responsibly fulfilled their governance role. This has resulted in legal obligations and codes of practice regarding their responsibilities and functioning. For example, it is the trustees of a charity, rather than the chief executive, who have the ultimate responsibility for ensuring that it is compliant with charitable law and fulfils its stated objectives. The external environment is also important. Again the examples above highlight that even if a Partnership Board is successfully managing its own internal functioning it will struggle to have an impact if other local bodies are unclear or unwelcoming of its work. Similarly, national policy may change over time and other developments be introduced which undermine its role.

These challenges to successful board operation have led academics to develop different schools of theories regarding the fundamental principles on which they operate (Chambers et al. 2013). *Principal-agent* theory suggests that boards are there to direct and control the resources available because there is a danger that staff will behave in the way that promotes their own self-interest rather than in the interests of the organisation. *Stewardship theory* takes the starting point that people within an organisation can be trusted to behave in an ethical manner in line with the agreed values. From this perspective, the role of a board is not to direct but work alongside the wider staff group and provide strategic direction due to their knowledge of the external environment and what may develop in the future. A third is that the role of the board is primarily to manage the relationship between the organisation and its stakeholders. This was developed in recognition that the previous focus on the board's relationship with 'shareholders' did not reflect either the realities of modern business or that public organisations do not have shareholders as such. Stakeholder theory instead recommends that boards are aware of all the groups that have a 'stake' in the organisation and that they seek to understand, respond and manage the trade-offs between these interests. These theories (and there are many others!) present quite different starting points of how a board, both within an organisation or of a partnership, should discharge its duties. As ever no theories will provide all the insights that are required but all of them help in some way to understand the possibility and limitations of a Partnership Board.

Integrated organisations

Organisations direct their staff members as to how they should prioritise their time and other resources. This includes setting out the limit of their responsibilities and how the funding available to the organisation can be used. This in turn can lead to gaps and disputes between organisations about who will meet the needs of someone which lie between what they view as their core responsibilities. Bringing together services into a single organisation therefore appears to provide constructive means to address many of these problems. Organisations outside of the field of integrated care are also interested in developing single entities that bring together previously separate organisations. This is commonly called the process of 'mergers' or 'acquisition'. The former implies that two or more peer organisations have decided to come together in order to derive shared benefits, whereas the latter implies that a stronger organisation has essentially bought another one. Whilst these are perhaps most common in private business, there are also numerous examples of such mergers in public service too.

Whatever the sector, there is a common set of assumptions about the potential value of mergers and acquisitions. The first is that bringing together the organisations will bring about economies of scale. The organisations may for example have their own human resources, finance and information technology departments. Combining these should enable efficiencies to be achieved through removing duplication in management or separate external contracts. The second is that they will be able to draw on the diverse skills and resources within the organisations to develop an improved offer or product to the external environment. It may be for example that one company has expertise of a new innovation that the other company recognises is important but does not have the necessary experience or competence to produce. A third is that by coming together (and this is particularly the case in acquisitions) an organisation can reduce the competition that it experiences for resources by taking over a rival.

How could integrated organisations provide more integrated care?

A single organisation will mean that all the professionals and services are employed and held to account by a single governing body. This enables the organisation to require them to work to the same policies, procedures and corporate values. The single organisation will be motivated to address gaps in provision in which there is uncertainty about who has responsibility as these will now fall under its remit.

Health and Social Care Trusts

Following devolution in 1999 there was a review of the health and social care structures within Northern Ireland. At that point there were 18 delivery organisations of which eleven were responsible for integrated health and social care services. The review decided to maintain the tradition of structural integration but to amalgamate the existing organisations into five comprehensive organisations responsible for hospital, community health and social care services. This includes social work services, residential care homes and day centres alongside health centres and community hospitals (see Box 7.3). A sixth trust is responsible for ambulance services.

Box 7.3 Belfast Health and Social Care Trust

Belfast Trust delivers care and treatment to approximately 340,000 people and provides a number of specialist services across the country. In 2015–16 it delivered 5,961 babies, saw 135,505 attendances in accident and emergency, provided 10,000 hours of home care per week and was corporate parent to 740 looked after children. Launched on 1 April 2007 following the merger of six existing trusts, it employs over 20,000 staff and has an annual budget of £1.3 billion. The trust is supported by a charity which provides funding for activities such as medical research, improving the building and environment, patient education and welfare, and purchasing new equipment. A group of trustees is responsible for overseeing the charity which had assets of about £50 million in March 2018.

Purpose: To improve health and wellbeing and reduce health and social inequalities.

Vision: To continuously improve health and social care delivery and foster innovation in pursuit of this goal. We will seek to achieve the right balance between providing more health and social care in, or closer to, people's homes and supporting the specialist delivery of acute care, thereby delivering positive outcomes for the people who use our services.

Board: The board is responsible for setting its strategic direction. It comprises a chairman, seven non-executive directors, five executive directors and seven other directors. Non-executive directors are appointed by the government. The chairman is accountable to the Minister of Health via the Permanent Secretary at the Department of Health, Social Services and Public Safety. The board holds the executive team to account for the operational management of the trust.

Structure: Five service directorates: Acute Services, Cancer and Specialist Services, Adult Social and Primary Care Services (including Mental Health and Learning Disability), Specialist Hospitals and Women's Health and Children's Community Services.

Delivering health and social care within a single organisational structure in Northern Ireland has been seen to deliver a range of benefits (Ham et al. 2013). Funding is allocated to programmes of work in which the managers can use the available resources flexibly across health and social care services. There is an emphasis on 'parity of esteem' between professions and management roles are open to those from different professions. These benefits have enabled the introduction of efficient processes relating to transition points such as hospital discharge. However, health, and in particular medical, services are seen to dominate through their allocation of resources and the overall paradigm of care. This means that social care is seen to be lacking in profile and invest-ment. Professional education continues to be delivered separately and there are still issues regarding stereotyping and perceived differences in status.

Care Trusts

Care Trusts were introduced in England through the NHS Plan in 2000. They were part of an overall strategy to improve partnership working between health and social care. Local authorities could delegate funding, staff and responsibility for social care services to the NHS body. It was hoped that a single organisation would enable 'tailored and integrated care, greater accessibility, and one stop shops for services that used to entail repeated conversations and a procession of different faces at times of illness, stress and vulnerability' (Department of Health 2002, p1). With the approval of the Secretary of State, Care Trusts could take on responsibility for delivering health and social care services and/or the role of commissioning and purchasing community based provision (see Box 7.4). Around half of Care Trusts delivered services for people with a mental health and/or learning disability with the rest com-missioning and/or providing general community health and social care services.

Box 7.4 Torbay Care Trust (Lavender 2006; Thistlethwaite 2011)

Torbay is an area on the south coast of England. Due to its popularity as a retirement destination it had a higher than average number of older people. Adult Social Services were not performing well in the early 2000s which was also nega-tively affecting the delivery of health care services. It was

---

therefore decided to better align community health and social work teams through configuring them in 'zones' based around clusters of general practices. One of the zones, Brixham, was selected to develop a more integrated model. Community nurses, social workers, occupational therapists and other staff were moved into new inter-professional teams under the direction of a single general manager. Health and social care coordinators were then appointed to streamline the assessment and coordination processes.

Following the success of the pilot, the model was introduced across the Torbay area with the Care Trust providing a legal basis for the development. This involved most of the adult social care staff working in the council being transferred to the NHS. The vision of the Care Trust was based around a fictional character called 'Mrs Smith'. This was developed on the basis of engagement with older people living in the area and reflected the common problems that were faced by people who required support from multiple services. These were used to consider how new approaches could improve the experience of people such as Mrs Smith. Evaluations of Torbay Care Trust suggested that there was considerable improvement in the delivery of health and social care, including reductions in delays in transfer of care, fewer uses of emergency beds by older people and increased use of direct payments. The merger was also seen to provide management savings and enable better integration of patient and client recording systems.

Despite governmental aspirations that they would become the predominant vehicle for delivering community-based health and social care services only 12 Care Trusts were in fact developed. The ones which commissioned health and social care services were disbanded by 2011 due to the Transforming Community

Service policy in which health care organisations were no longer able to both purchase and deliver services. Mental health Care Trusts have continued as organisations although not all now are still responsible for social care services. Interviews with senior managers within Care Trusts suggested that there were advantages from bringing social care into a single entity (Miller et al. 2011). This included benefits in relation to staffing (redesigning roles to reflect needs of local people and providing greater diversity of career paths), service development (to build on the best of health and social care), coordination (sharing of information and creation of joint teams) and wider partnerships (larger organisations had greater influence and were a focal point for community engagement). Most would not though have created a single organisation in hindsight. This was because they thought that the value could have been achieved more simply through other means. Merging the staff and budgets into a single organisation involved considerable complications including bringing together different terms and conditions, a distancing from the council of social care services, and social care staff groups feeling dominated and under-valued.

Discussion

It is clear from wider research that the benefits expected from merging any large organisation are rarely achieved as quickly as is hoped. This appears to be due to a lack of recognition of the many complexities involved and a tendency for those initiating the change to take an optimistic perspective on outcomes and timelines. Furthermore, there is evidence that such a major change can have negative consequences. It is common for staff to feel higher levels of stress, uncertainty about their future employment and frustration with a lack of unified processes (Fulop et al. 2005). With sufficient time it appears that benefits can be achieved in some circumstances. One study found that after three years staff reported that mergers of NHS organisations had led to greater autonomy, improved professional supervision and better career prospects. Recent mergers of NHS trusts in England were also thought to result in some improvements. These included greater efficiency in service delivery through streamlining management structures and consolidating delivery onto fewer sites, process improvement through introducing the best of the pathways in place across the organisations, and easier recruitment through professionals being attracted to a single organisation of greater depth and scale.

It is clear that the transition process deployed in the merger is crucial to the benefits being realised (Miller & Millar 2017). Again the issues are similar whichever organisations are being brought together. Within integrated care the considerable diversity of professions and backgrounds will bring added issues. There may not have been a good working relationship between the organisations and their staff prior to this point. A clear articulation of the benefits is crucial, with detailed planning of how to realise these benefits before the organisations come together. Engaging stakeholders inside and external to the organisation helps to highlight areas of concern, identify opportunities to improve and explain the rationale for the merger. A common culture must be developed within the new organisation. In cases of 'mergers of equals' this should involve a new culture being created, but if it is essentially a 'take over' then it may be better for the culture of the stronger organisation to be transferred to the other. If this is the case, then it should be made clear and not promoted as a merger of equals as staff prefer transparency and honesty. Finally, there must be a realism about what can be achieved – setting unachievable expectations will lead to frustration and disillusionment (Aldwych Partners 2016).

Pooled budgets

Resources are a major source of tension between organisations. For providers this may be related to formally competing for tenders to deliver services or lobbying public sector bodies to prioritise the populations and services for which they have responsibility. There are also many situations in which providers may perceive that another organisation is not fulfilling its responsibilities which results in the provider having to take on activities that it sees as outside its remit. Public sector organisations which commission services face the challenge of too many demands on the funding available. Similar to providers, they will traditionally have strongly challenged other commissioners if it is perceived that they are neglecting or shifting responsibilities. Such funding disputes can lead to considerable delay in people receiving services as the organisations concerned try to negotiate what they see as a fair settlement. This can also result in people remaining in more expensive services as the alternatives would come under the funding remit of an alternative organisation.

How could pooled budgets help provide more integrated care?

Organisations will tend to be protective of the budget that they have been allocated for a population. They will see this as being necessary for them to deliver their responsibilities and be reluctant to share this with other organisations in case these are no longer achieved. Bringing the available funding together into a single budget can help to remove such individual interests as the money loses its organisational identity. This could then encourage organisations to think collectively about how best all of the resources for the population could be used to ensure more integrated care.

Better Care Fund

The Better Care Fund (initially known as the Integration Transformation Fund) was announced in England in 2013. It would create a

> single pooled budget for health and social care services to work more closely together in local areas, based on a plan agreed between the NHS and local authorities ... with the aim of delivering better, more joined-up services to older and

disabled people, to keep them out of hospital and to avoid long hospital stays.

(HM Treasury 2013, p22)

The fund was largely comprised of funding that was already allocated by central government to local health and social care bodies. This included disabled facilities grants, social care capital money, carers breaks funding and reablement grants. Local areas had to pool this money into a single pot across health and social care. The mandated elements in 2015–16 came to £3.8 billion. Funding would be released in stages dependent on areas demonstrating sufficient progress in implementation and performance.

Local areas could also choose to pool more than the minimum required, and in 2015–16 this led to another £1.5 billion being pooled. Health and Wellbeing Boards were tasked with developing jointly agreed plans which set out the services and projects they would support and how these would fulfil the national conditions and performance indicators. In total 4,216 activities/schemes were included in the plans (Forder et al. 2018). Thirty per cent of the total spend was on intermediate care and 25 per cent on protecting social care.

Box 7.5 National conditions for Better Care Fund (2015–16)

Plans jointly agreed by health and wellbeing board members.
Protect existing social care services.
Seven-day working in health and social care.
Better data sharing between health and social care.
An accountable professional for integrated packages of care.
Agree the impact of the plan on the health and social care providers.

Local plans for the Better Care Fund were submitted to regional NHSE England and local government representatives for review (NAO 2014). These initially assessed that 90 per cent of plans were good enough to be approved. However, moderation of plans by central government raised significant concerns that the expected level of savings would be realised. One problem was that the amount that each local area would be expected to contribute to the target sum (£1 billion) had not been clearly communicated. This led to changes in the design of the programme. The pay for performance element was now solely focused on reductions in the number of emergency admissions. Other national mechanisms to improve the working of the fund were put in place including webinars, expert clinics to review draft plans and direct support from consultants for areas which were most struggling. Additional funding was subsequently added to the fund including £2 billion in 2017 to help shore up adult social care. There was a reduction in national conditions to four aspects – signing off by the Health and Wellbeing Board, maintaining social care services, investing in out-of-hospital services and implementing a nationally developed High Impact Change Model for Managing Transfer of Care.

The National Audit Office review of emergency admission reduction in 2018 reported the Better Care Fund was demonstrating limited progress in achieving these reductions. Most areas were not meeting their own targets (NAO 2018). However, the fund was found to have reduced delayed transfers of care by 9.3 per cent. Local case study sites reported that the additional funding was welcome but the restrictions on its use prevented them for using it in the way that they would choose. Sites also suggested other challenges, including tensions between partners on how to prioritise and manage the spend, 'competition' from other policy initiatives and national metrics capturing a limited set of outcomes (Forder et al. 2018)

Whole Place Community Budgets

Since 2001 there have been a series of initiatives in England which have sought to encourage local areas to take a more collaborative approach to the used of their individual resources. This includes local strategic partnerships, local area agreements and the Total Place pilots. Whilst these did not deliver all of the expected outcomes and savings the belief has continued that it should be possible to achieve better results with a pooling of resources. The Department for Communities and Local Government launched a related pilot programme in October 2011. Local areas were invited to express an interest in exploring the potential of a 'whole-place' community budget. There was not a set structure or focus for the budgets but there were suggestions as to what the pilots might consider. This included the outcomes that would be achieved, how they could be governed and what methodologies would help to assess the costs and benefits of the potential options. The overall message was that the pilots should be about new ways of working rather than a financial process per se, with an emphasis on being preventative, focused on the person and drawing investment from a range of partners.

Four areas were selected to be pilots: Cheshire West and Chester, Essex, Greater Manchester and Tri-borough in London (Table 7.1). It was estimated that if their proposals were successfully implemented and rolled out across England there could be up to £20.6 billion of annual savings (LGIU 2013). The areas which were seen to have the most potential for efficiencies were health and social care, work and skills, and supporting families with complex needs. New approaches connected with the greater pooling of resources were varied (LGA 2013). Tri-borough introduced a new contracting and reimbursement approach that funded health and social care providers on the basis of what a patient receives in totality rather than on the basis of specific procedures. Greater Manchester supported troubled families through key-working, dedicated workers with small caseloads, shared IT to enable early identification of families at risk and to track their progress, and leadership from a multi-agency steering group. Cheshire West and Chester believed that the incidence and harm from domestic violence could be reduced through a dedicated access team, a common assessment process and a range of interventions for perpetrators such as electronic monitoring, violence awareness programmes and addressing substance misuse.

Table 7.1 Pilot sites within the Whole Place Community Budget programme (NAO 2013)

Whole Place pilot site	Activities within the pilot	Anticipated economic benefits
Cheshire West and Chester	Assertive case management support for troubled families; addressing the causes of domestic violence; supporting job seekers to be ready for work; reducing hospital admissions for older people	£56 million net savings over five years
Essex	Employer-led remodelling of vocational skills; reducing offending and supporting families of offenders; integrating health and social care; reducing domestic violence; supporting families with complex needs through a nominated worker	£414 million in net savings over six years
Greater Manchester	Early years, transforming justice, troubled families, health and social care	£270 million net savings over five years
Tri-borough in London	Reducing use of hospitals through investment in community health and social care; focusing reoffending services on short-stay prisoners; supporting troubled families; delivering new construction jobs through building of new homes	£70 million net savings annually

Discussion

Structural integration of budgets is included in many of the reforms that have been introduced across the UK. This reflects international thinking on the centrality of disputes about funding to problems of fragmented care. An evidence review of the benefits of pooling funding across health and social care was published in 2015 (Mason et al. 2015). This reports that over half of the 38 schemes which had been researched did not find any improvements in health outcomes. Thirty-four projects considered impacts on the use of hospital care which is often seen as a major opportunity to improve cost effectiveness. Three of studies found that there had been reductions in the secondary care activity but the remainder either found no significant effect or a mixture of both increases and decreases. Even if there was support or indeed encouragement for local organisations to pool their funds from national government it proved a complicated and difficult undertaking. Bringing the money together did not address other barriers such as incompatible information sharing systems, alternative performance frameworks and clashes in organisational cultures. Integration of budgets was though linked with improving access to care. Whilst this could lead to increased use of resources in the short term it did help to address inequities of care and may result in better health and wellbeing in the long term. Integrating of budgets should therefore be seen as one enabler rather than as a cure-all solution to achieve more coordinated care.

Partnership Boards commonly hold public meetings. Identify one in your local area which is responsible for a population and/or issue of interest for you. Attend a meeting to observe how it fulfils its role. This includes not only the content of its discussions, but also how the meeting is run and the interactions between the members. Consider too who is not included, and what in your view is missing from the agenda.

Further resources

National Audit Offices

England: www.nao.org.uk **Northern Ireland:** www.niauditoffice. gov.uk **Scotland:** www.audit-scotland.gov.uk **Wales:** www.audit. wales

Government bodies which undertake independent audits of progress with national policies and the connected use of resources. Excellent sources of recent reviews of the implementation of integrated care strategies.

214 Integrating across a system

Organisation for Economic Co-operation and Development
www.oecd.org/health

International body that seeks to help countries achieve high-performing health systems by measuring health outcomes and the use of health system resources as well as by analysing policies that improve access, efficiency and quality of health care.

References

Aldwych Partners. (2016). *Benefits from mergers: lessons from recent NHS transactions*. Available at: https://improvement.nhs.uk/resources/how-make-nhs-mergers-work-better-patients/ (downloaded 05.11.2018)

Audit Scotland. (2011). *Review of Community Health Partnerships*. Available at: www.audit-scotland.gov.uk/docs/health/2011/nr_110602_chp.pdf (downloaded 05.11.2018)

CCISW. (2011). *Joint inspection of Local Safeguarding Children Boards*. Available at: www.justiceinspectorates.gov.uk/probation/wp-content/uploads/sites/5/2014/03/joint-inspection-local-safeguarding-children-boards-2011.pdf (downloaded 05.11.2018)

Chambers, N., Harvey, G., Mannion, R., Bond, J., & Marshall, J. (2013). *Towards a framework for enhancing the performance of NHS boards: a synthesis of the evidence about board governance, board effectiveness and board development*. Available at: www.ncbi.nlm.nih.gov/books/NBK259411/ (downloaded 05.11.2018)

Department of Health. (2002). *Care Trusts: background briefing*. London: Department of Health.

Forder, J., Caiels, J., Harlock, J., Wistow, G., Malisauskaite, G., Peters, M., ... Jones, K. (2018). *A system-level evaluation of the Better Care Fund*. Available at: www.pssru.ac.uk/pub/5424.pdf (downloaded 08.11.2018)

Fulop, N., Protopsaltis, G., King, A., Allen, P., Hutchings, A., & Normand, C. (2005). Changing organisations: a study of the context and processes of mergers of health care providers in England. *Social Science & Medicine, 60*(1), 119–130.

Ham, C., Heenan, D., Longley, M., & Steel, D. (2013) *Integrated care in Northern Ireland, Scotland and Wales. Lessons for England*. Available at: www.kingsfund.org.uk/sites/default/files/field/field_publication_file/integrated-care-in-northern-ireland-scotland-and-wales-kingsfund-jul13.pdf (downloaded 05.11.2018)

HM Treasury. (2013). *Spending round 2013*. Available at: www.gov.uk/government/publications/spending-round-2013-documents (downloaded 08.11.2018)

Laming, H. (2003). *The Victoria Climbie Inquiry*. Available at: www.gov.uk/government/publications/the-victoria-climbie-inquiry-report-of-an-inquiry-by-lord-laming (downloaded 04.11.2018)

Laming, H. (2009). *The protection of children in England: a progress report*. Available at: www.gov.uk/government/publications/the-protection-of-children-in-england-a-progress-report (downloaded 05.11.2018)

Lavender, A. (2006). Creation of a Care Trust: managing the project. *Journal of Integrated Care, 14*(5), 14–22.

LGIU. (2013). *Whole-place community budgets an LGiU essential guide*. Available at: www.lgiu.org.uk/wp-content/uploads/2013/04/Whole-place-community-budgets-an-lgiu-essential-guide.pdf (downloaded 08.11.2018)

Local Government Association. (2013). *Local public service transformation: a guide to Whole Place Community Budgets*. Available at: www.communityplanningtoolkit.org/sites/default/files/WholePlaceCommunityBudgets.pdf (downloaded 08.11.2018).

Mason, A., Goddard, M., Weatherly, H., & Chalkley, M. (2015). Integrating funds for health and social care: an evidence review. *Journal of Health Services Research & Policy, 20*(3), 177–188.

Miller, R., Dickinson, H., & Glasby, J. (2011). The care trust pilgrims. *Journal of Integrated Care, 19*(4), 14–21.

Miller, R., & Millar, R. (2017). *Partnering for Improvement: inter-organisational developments in the NHS*. Birmingham: HSMC. Available at: www.birmingham.ac.uk/Documents/college-social-sciences/social-policy/HSMC/news-events/2017/final-report-part nering-for-improvement-august-2017.pdf (downloaded 05.11. 2018).

Munro, E. (2012). *The Munro Review of Child Protection: progress report: moving towards a child centred system*. Available at: www.gov.uk/government/publications/progress-report-moving-towards-a-child-centred-system (downloaded 05.11.2018)

National Assembly for Wales Health, Wellbeing and Local Government Committee. (2010). *Inquiry into Local Safeguarding Children Boards in Wales*. Available at: www.assembly.wales/en/bus-home/bus-third-assembly/3-committees/pages/committeeitem. aspx?category=HWLG&itemid=3146 (downloaded 05.11.2018)

National Audit Office. (2013). *Case study on integration: measuring the costs and benefits of Whole-Place Community Budgets*. Available at: www.nao.org.uk/report/case-study-on-integration-measuring-the-costs-and-benefits-of-whole-place-community-budgets/ (downloaded 08.11.2018)

National Audit Office. (2014). *Planning for the Better Care Fund*. Available at: www.nao.org.uk/wp-content/uploads/2014/11/Plan ning-for-the-better-care-fund.pdf (downloaded 08.11.2018)

National Audit Office. (2018). *Reducing emergency admissions*. Available at: www.nao.org.uk/report/reducing-emergency-admis sions/ (downloaded 08.11.2018)

Thistlethwaite, P. (2011). *Integrating health and social care in Torbay*. London: The King's Fund.

Wood, A. (2016). *Wood review of local safeguarding children boards*. Available at: www.gov.uk/government/publications/wood-review-of-local-safeguarding-children-boards (downloaded 05.11.2018)

8 Where next for integrated care?

Expectations are high in all the home nations regarding the potential of integrated care to achieve better outcomes for people, improve the wellbeing of communities and make more efficient use of public resources. This reflects thinking in most developed nations on the need for social care, health, housing and education services to collaborate more effectively. Knowledge of the factors that encourage (and prevent) people experiencing integrated care is steadily growing. The numerous implementation programmes in the United Kingdom, across Europe and in many parts of the world are generating insights on approaches to bring together professionals, services and organisations around the needs of individuals and populations. There are new research tools for measuring the outcomes of integrated care and frameworks for tracking the process of transformation. Associated journals, practice guidance and web-based resources are growing in number and depth of content. There are numerous opportunities to engage with professionals across the United Kingdom and internationally through conferences, on-line networks and social media. Now, more than ever, the time is right for integrated care to become the norm.

Despite this progress it is apparent that there is still some way to go before fragmented care is eradicated. The divisions within welfare services are firmly established within organisational cultures and professional practice. Austerity has in some cases encouraged new ways of working to address common shortfalls but more typically has resulted in organisations taking control of their boundaries in order to hang onto their dwindling resources. As is often the case, it is those who are already discriminated against and disadvantaged who are affected most by these increasing tensions and gaps in services. Integrated care is therefore more pressing than ever if further harm and inequalities are to be avoided. This will require greater understanding of what approaches are best deployed in what circumstances, and how best to sustain new developments into the long term. In this concluding chapter, three promising areas of innovation in thinking, delivery and organisation for integrated care are considered.

The famous work by Rogers (2003) suggests that people's willingness to adopt new innovations can be divided into four categories – early adopters (who engage when the innovation is largely unknown and its impacts uncertain), early majority (who participate when the initial teething problems have been addressed and there are positive reports emerging), late majority (who adopt when the innovation looks as if it is going to continue into the long term) and the laggards (who resist acceptance until well after most other people have already implemented). How would you generally place yourself on this continuum? What influences the speed with which you would adopt an innovation? It is also worth noting that laggards may be out of step with the majority but can have excellent grounds for refusing to accept the mainstream view.

System leadership

It will be evident that many of the barriers to providing more integrated care relate to organisations and professions maintaining historic patterns of behaviour. These may have served well in previous times to achieve more limited objectives but are not able to respond to the complexity of the modern era or to deliver more holistic and person-centred outcomes. Moving beyond these traditional approaches and the relationships which support them requires not only considerable effort but also fundamentally new ways of thinking. Achieving such a new vision has been conceptualised as requiring leadership rather than management – 'the business of management is to strengthen the as it is, the challenge of leadership is to create what else the system can be' (Oshry 1999). Management involves the direct control of resources which largely stop at boundaries related to organisations, contractual specifications or professional roles. When times are difficult it is common for managers to respond through exerting greater control and strengthening the boundaries around their services and organisations to protect their existing resources. For example, access criteria may be tightened and there may be a withdrawal from joint projects that are seen as 'nice to have' but not essential to achieving their core performance targets. Integrated care however requires contributions from a diversity of professions and services which may not be in any sense organised into a coherent whole and greater flexibility in how resources are used (Welbourn et al. 2012). This relates to the concept of complexity that we discussed in Chapter 3.

Leadership is the art of inspiring others to follow a course of action not on the basis that this is mandated by terms of employment but because they are motivated by its underpinning vision and values. Much of its work is about providing new ways to frame situations which then enable others to see an aspect of the world differently and thereby commit to alternative behaviours and relationships. Systems leadership is 'leadership across organisational and geopolitical boundaries, beyond individual professional disciplines, within a range of organisational and stakeholder cultures ... [in order to] effect change for positive social benefit across multiple interacting and intersecting systems' (Ghate et al. 2013, p13). Senge et al. (2015) describe three core capabilities of such leadership – an ability to see the larger system and help others to move beyond individual and limited viewpoints, encouraging shared reflection in which people collectively consider thinking and feelings other than their own to develop trust and a deeper understanding, and to use anxieties and dissatisfaction with current realities to generate a shared inspiring vision for the future. It has been described as involving six interrelated dimensions (see Box 8.1).

**Box 8.1 Dimensions of systems leadership
(Ghate et al. 2013)**

Ways of feeling: defining and demonstrating core values that inspire others and which encourage them to commit to new ways of working and collaborating with each other.

Ways of perceiving: not only having a higher view than those involved in day-to-day delivery but also recognising that as system leaders even they are not able to observe all the elements and connections. This requires working positively with such uncertainty and listening to other voices.

Ways of thinking: interpreting the complexity and ambiguity to identify the central issues and then translating these into forms that could be understood by others.

Ways of relating: building and maintaining relationships with others through empathy, transparency and authenticity.

Ways of doing: stimulating, facilitating and enabling others to undertake actions through creating an environment that encourages innovation and creativity.

Ways of being: demonstrating personal qualities such as bravery, drive, resilience, humility and patience.

All of the home nations have recognised the importance of systems leadership to achieving more integrated care. The Health and Sport Committee of the Scottish Parliament reviewed progress with integration as part of the preparatory work for the health budget in 2019–20. It concluded that if integration were to deliver transformational change there would need to be 'fundamental changes in the relationship between local authorities and health boards' (Scottish Government Health & Sport Committee 2018, p18). Achieving this would require strong leadership within the Integration Authorities. The committee therefore recommended that the Scottish government evaluate their leadership competence and provide support when it was seen to be insufficient. One of the five whole system values within the Welsh government vision for the future of health and social care is the 'driving of transformative change through strong leadership .... more open and confident engagement with external partners' (Welsh Government 2018, p4). The learning summaries from the new models of care programme highlight that 'effective leadership is a critical enabler for change' (LGA et al. 2018, p8). One example provided is that of Wakefield. The vanguard was seeking in particular to provide more integrated care for people within care homes. The chief executives of the local organisations took on specific system leadership roles that were often outside their areas of expertise. This modelled their expectation that professionals would also be asked to take on new responsibilities.

This emphasis on systems leadership to support integrated care is replicated in other countries. The World Health Organisation (2015) describes implementation of integrated care strategies as requiring

> *transformational leadership* that goes beyond understanding how to bring together stakeholders with competing views and mind-sets, but which pro-actively communicates the goals and values of the strategy and seeks to mobilize others through a more emotional involvement in the need for change ...
>
> (p35)

The Toronto Central Community Care Access Centre has multiple awards in relation to the improvements in care for populations with complex needs. The team responsible for overseeing the programme reflected on their experiences of undertaking such change. They identified three main areas of learning which reflect the principles of systems leadership: the need to change the conversation from organisations focusing on themselves to discussing what people and families want; reflective conversations between partners about what is working and what is not to enable trust and shared meaning; and being willing to let initiatives evolve over time through rapid testing rather than sticking to a fixed model. They conclude that 'fundamental changes to how care is structured and delivered demand "system leaders" with leadership competencies that support effective and sustainable relationship development among traditionally disparate components' (Evans et al. 2016, p35).

Having recognised the importance of systems leadership, defined its concepts and identified its constituent parts, the issue is how to develop it in practice. The Systems Leadership Alliance was developed by a partnership of health and social care organisations in England. It provides practical and expert support to enable new leadership behaviours to be developed and sustained. One of its programmes is the Local Vision Initiative in which localities are paired with an 'enabler' who has many years of experience in implementing change, innovation and systems thinking. Participants also attended whole programme learning network events hosted at the Kings Fund. Local projects have sought to address a wide diversity of complex problems. These include low levels of school age children participating in sports or physical activity, the risk of female genital mutilation amongst girls and young women, and the difficulties that some communities have in accessing affordable and fresh food (Vize 2014). The evaluation suggests that despite its modest budget the programme has been able to facilitate a shared and more inclusive approach to leadership in the local areas. Enablers provided not only expertise but also informed and constructive challenge to existing thinking and relationships. Their skills, and their ability to adapt their style to the local context were therefore central to positive outcomes. Active commitment by local partners to the programme was necessary to align with other initiatives and to ensure that local teams had access to resources and project management (Bolden et al. 2015).

The Advancing Quality Alliance (AQuA) is an improvement network in the north west of England. Reflecting the uncertainties about how best leaders should respond to complex issues, it created Integrated Care Discovery Communities which brought together local leaders to test out new ideas (Fillingham & Weir 2014). AQuA provided direct support to the areas regarding their integrated care initiatives alongside helping them to develop their own capability and skills. The learning programmes were co-produced with participants to ensure that these reflected their priorities and thoughts. Common themes emerged across the groups. These were – the importance of having a space to learn, the unifying power of focusing on place and a need for insatiable curiosity. It was important for such development to not only be provided for senior managers and clinicians, but also at the micro (teams and localities) and the meso (services and patients pathways) levels.

New technologies

Technology is sometimes linked with being a barrier to more integrated care due to the equipment or data within different organisations being unable to connect successfully. Technology is of course advancing continually with new forms providing emerging opportunities for improving communication and coordination. Digital, and the information that it can enable, is seen as having a particular role in facilitating more integrated care. This relates to people, professionals and systems (see Box 8.2). There are examples of how such impacts have been realised in practice. The Connecting Care programme in the south west of England is a partnership between 17 organisations. This includes councils, hospitals and community health providers. The system is able to draw on the individual record systems within each organisation (a total of 14 such systems) to compile a single data record for each person. Professionals can view this data on a 'need to know' basis and it is updated in real time. Initially focused on adults, Connecting Care has been extended to services for children. This could in the future enable education services and the police to integrate their data in relation to children and families (Local Government Association & IPC 2016). NHS Highland have been creating a single e-record for each person which will bring together their data from social care as well as primary, secondary and community health care. It is planned to include within the system functionality that would enable professionals to have dialogues about a person. This could potentially save the person being asked to visit another service and provide them with necessary support at an earlier point. The vision is to then further integrate these records on a regional basis with Grampian, Orkney and Shetland (NHS Highland 2018, www.connectingcarebnssg.co.uk/).

Box 8.2 Potential contribution of digital technology to integrated care (Local Government Association & IPC 2016)

- People can connect with services through channels with which they feel comfortable and in a time and place to suit their lifestyle
- People can access and manage their own information which will enable them to be better informed and share current details with the relevant professionals
- People will be supported to make decisions over their wellbeing through understanding
- Professional can access information that people have shared with other services and organisations
- Professionals can see a single and joined up view of the person's needs and the support that they are receiving
- Systems can develop shared platforms which identify and explain the range of resources available
- Systems can pool data such as outcomes, demand and activity across sectors to enable more informed commissioning

---

Digital solutions have already been introduced which are primarily focused on people and their families. ALISS (A Local Information System for Scotland) was developed in 2009. The Scottish Government had recognised that better supporting people in managing long-term conditions would require them to have better information about how to maintain their wellbeing. The potential of asset-based approaches was also being highlighted by (amongst others) the Chief Medical Officer of Scotland. ALISS was to respond to both these opportunities through being a vehicle by which people could connect with their communities and with each other in order to provide and access assets. The team responsible was aware of the danger of such a system being cumbersome, slow to respond and unfriendly to people who were unfamiliar with such processes. They therefore designed ALISS with the active participation of people and communities. This included workshops with adult learners at a literacy class, individual discussions with people with complex conditions and engagement events bringing together people, professionals, policy makers and designers (Alliance Scotland 2013). This resulted in ALISS gathering together details of local community and statutory resources and making this list available to people (and professionals) through many different access points. This could be a physical location such as a general practice or library, or could be through existing websites that people would be viewing. Services and individuals can upload and update information directly. In January 2016 there were around 11,500 searches on average per month. The service has been used by other initiatives such as the National Links Worker Programme. The Links Workers access the information from ALISS on behalf of the people they are supporting and also encourage them to engage directly (Alliance Scotland 2016).

Beyond these existing technologies are emerging developments which are being explored in relation to public services. Many of these have potential applications in relation to more integrated care.

Robots: Prototypes have been developed of robots which can assist people in maintaining their independence and enjoying a better quality of life (Consilium Research & Consultancy 2018). Physically assistive robots will undertake care-related tasks such as lifting and carrying someone who is unable to support their own weight. This could be carried out independently or in conjunction with a family or paid carers. Socially assistive robots facilitate people's engagement with activities related to their wellbeing such as remembering to drink or to take medication. They can provide comfort and stimulation through being programmed to interact with someone, including those with cognitive difficulties such as dementia. Robots could promote integrated care through reminding or connecting people with the various members of their care team. They could be pro-grammed to undertake direct tasks that have been traditionally undertaken by a number of professionals – for example nurses, home carers and physiotherapists.

Artificial intelligence: Computers are being programmed to under-take functions that would usually be seen as requiring intelli-gence by people such as using language and learning from experiences. Artificial intelligence is seen as having considerable potential within diagnostic processes (Castle-Clarke 2018). This involves creating algorithms that enable the computer to analyse data from scans of the human body. Primary care services are using 'deep-learning' algorithms (i.e. those that build and evolve as they gather more data) to guide people via on-line portals. Once the person has entered their symptoms, they are advised which service(s) or course of action is the most appropriate. Robots could use artificial intelligence to gather data from someone's condition (including their levels of anxiety) through body sensors which could then be used to learn how their interactions can improve wellbeing (Consilium Research & Consultancy 2018). Such developments could improve integrated care through creating on-line platforms that can direct people to the breadth of services which may be relevant and available in their area.

Big data: Social work, health, education and other services already generate considerable amounts of data related to activity, spend and assessed need. Through new mobile apps people also directly contribute data on their mental and physical wellbeing. In principle this data could be an invaluable tool for identifying gaps or duplications in services and predicting what capacity and connections will be required in the future. Data sets that are held within sectors and different levels of govern-ment would though have to be made compatible. Undoubtedly there will be a need for robust processes to ensure that data is accurate and up to date. The concerns of many people regarding their personal data, and in particular if it is to be shared outside of public services, will need to be addressed too (Castle-Clarke 2018).

Realising the potential of new technologies within public services is though notoriously difficult. A review of technology and innovation in health and social care by the Scottish Parliament in 2018 was hoping to find out more about 'ways of modernising the health and social care sector through the use of modern technology and innovative and fresh ways of thinking' (Scottish Government Health & Sport Committee 2018, p29). Instead they found a 'culture that was reluctant to adapt and ... heavily outdated IT systems still cause major barriers' (ibid.). A scoping within social care in England found challenges relating to insufficient resources to implement the change, continued uncertainties over the legality of information sharing and poor inter-operability of systems (Local Government Association & IPC 2016). Ensuring that professionals have the technology and skills necessary to derive value from these opportunities is key. This is equally true for people, with a danger that they may suffer 'digital exclusion' in addition to other forms of inequality and isolation. The Home Nations have all recognised the importance and challenges of new technology within their future strategies for social work and other public services, including its potential benefits in better integrating care.

Accountable care

Many of the problems that must be overcome for people to experience integrated care are related to divisions between organisations and financial systems that do not encourage more collaborative working. As we have seen, initiatives such as partnership boards, pooling budgets and even merging services into a single organisation are limited at best in how they improve people's experience. Current thinking in some parts of the UK and many countries internationally is therefore that another level of integration is required that not only brings together organisations but also pays them to deliver more integrated care through contracts and incentive payments. These have been loosely described under the term 'accountable care organisations'. Models differ between and indeed within countries, but they are seen to have the following elements – they are responsible for the health and wellbeing of a defined population, care is managed across the continuum including prevention, crisis and long-term care and they are funded to take responsibility for both the quality and cost of caring for the population. This could be people living in a particular geography, or who have a similar condition, or are of a similar age. The term rose to prominence in the USA as part of the health reforms that were introduced by President Obama. Many of these were owned by doctors and/or private companies who were able to keep an element of cost reductions that were achieved.

There is considerable diversity between the forms of partnerships and how their funding is organised (see Box 8.3). Academics have therefore developed typologies which can be used to differentiate between them. McClellan et al. (2014) suggest there are five main domains to be considered – the population for which they are accountable, the outcomes that they must deliver, the metrics by which they will be monitored, the payment structures and incentives, and how they will better coordinate care. In England, the term Accountable Care was initially used to describe the future position for local systems in which there was good integration between health and social care organisations. The term was subsequently abandoned though due to concerns that it signalled an intent to engage private American health care corporations in the NHS. This was linked to the expectation that responsibility for taking on the role of lead organisation would be given following competitive tenders (see e.g. Pollock & Roderick 2018). There were also two challenges to the legality of such contracts from campaigning groups, but these were ultimately dismissed in court (see House of Commons 2018).

Box 8.3 Examples of Accountable Care related developments

Gesundes Kinzingtal (Peiris et al. 2018)

This partnership is responsible for the health of about 10,000 people in south-west Germany. It is led by jointly by a network of doctors and a health care company. These contract with care providers to deliver services with additional payments for those who take on care coordination and participation in quality improvement initiatives. Gesundes Kinzingtal seeks to promote wellbeing as well as respond to identified needs. It has partnerships with over 250 organisations and provides funding to community groups to run self-help groups, adult learning classes and sports facilities. Health promotion programmes are run within workplaces and schools. Four advisory groups (including two representing patients) guide its work.

Canterbury District Health Board (Gullery & Hamilton 2015; Charles 2017)

This is responsible for the planning and delivery of health and care services in the most populated region within the South Island of New Zealand. Due to a financial deficit, long waiting times for services and people remaining in hospital for extended periods it decided that a radical transformation was required. This was based on the notion that it would 'not waste people's time and would use funding in the best interests of the person' (Gullery & Hamilton 2015, p114). Alongside this vision of 'one system, one budget' it has invested in staff to encourage them to be innovative and has introduced an alliance contract which enables organisations to share the financial risks that can occur when a health and care system is being improved. These have led to a number of major initiatives to support integrated care

---

including rapid response teams for people who are acutely unwell in the community, single electronic health records and over 500 pathways setting out the care and support that people should receive. These are available electronically and provide accessible best practice guidance for professionals. The collaborative working within Canterbury contributed to its ability to respond to a massive earthquake in 2011.

Evidence to date regarding the impact of accountable care organisations is inconclusive. A Canadian review reported a better or at least maintained patient experience and achievement of individual clinical outcomes, mixed results in relation to addressing health inequalities and improving overall population health and some cost saving but often not as substantial as hoped (McMaster University 2016). A more recent review by an Australian research group similarly suggested there were modest savings but improvement in patient experience and quality of care (Peiris et al. 2018). McClellan et al. (2017) reflect on international experiences of accountable care to emphasise that developments of this nature require approaches that promote accountability for outcomes through collaboration and professional leadership, share data to enable more coordinated care for individuals and more informed strategic planning, and deploy multidisciplinary teams to engage professionals around people and their families. New forms of accountable care organisations are emerging. The United States government is investing in a holistic communities model which has greater emphasis on investing in community organisations to address social determinants of health such as housing, domestic violence and access to basics such as food and warmth. The associated programme will run for five years with flexibility for local areas to develop bespoke responses to these common challenges (Alley et al. 2016). Following the change of definition and legal challenges in England it would seem unlikely that there will be any integrated care vehicle for the foreseeable future labelled as 'accountable care'. However, there will undoubtedly be continued interest in new ways of configuring policy frameworks, funding streams and organisation relationships in response to the needs of populations.

Conclusion

More than ever, people, families and communities expect and need to experience integrated care. This will require continued commitment from national and local governments with associated investment and the bravery to challenge existing silos. Organisations require new partnerships with different sectors that seek creative solutions that move beyond established patterns of delivery. Professionals of all persuasions must be willing to understand and trust those from alternative disciplines and actively work towards mutual respect and relationships based on reciprocity.

Social workers have a professional duty to collaborate constructively around the needs of individuals and families. Furthermore, they are uniquely placed through their understanding of systems, their ability to work creatively with conflict, and their commitment to advocating for positive change. Social work is the profession of integration – now is the time for it to fulfill this potential.

Further resources

The Commonwealth Fund www.commonwealthfund.org

The Commonwealth Fund supports independent research on health care issues and making grants to improve health care practice and policy. An international programme in health policy is designed to stimulate innovative policies and practices in the United States and other industrialised countries.

Institute of Local Government Studies (INLOGOV) www.birming ham.ac.uk/schools/government-society/departments/local-govern ment-studies/index.aspx

INLOGOV is the leading academic centre for research and teaching on local governance and strategic public management. This includes system leadership and the future nature of public service.

The Health Foundation www.health.org.uk/about-us

The Health Foundation is an independent charity committed to bringing about better health and health care for people in the UK. The organisation's aim is a healthier population, supported by high quality care that can be equitably accessed.

References

Alley, D. E., Asomugha, C. N., Conway, P. H., & Sanghavi, D. M. (2016). Accountable health communities: addressing social needs through Medicare and Medicaid. *New England Journal of Medicine*, *374*(1), 8–11.

Alliance Scotland. (2013). *ALISS Access to Local Information to Support Self-management 2009–2013 report 1.* Available at: www.alliance-scotland.org.uk/wpcontent/uploads/2017/09/Alliance-ALISS-Report1.pdf3 (downloaded 15.11.2018)

Alliance Scotland. (2016). *ALISS Access to Local Information to Support Self-management 2013–2016 report 2.* Available at: www.alliancescotland.org.uk/digital/wp-content/uploads/2017/09/Alliance-ALISSReport2.pdf (downloaded 15.11.2018)

Bolden, R., Gulati, A., Ahmad, Y., Burgoyne, J., Chapman, N., Edwards, G., … Spirit, M. (2015). *The difference that makes the difference – final evaluation of the first place-based programmes for systems leadership: local vision. Project report*. Available from: http://eprints.uwe.ac.uk/27932 (downloaded 11.11.2018)

Castle-Clarke, S. (2018). *What will new technology mean for the NHS and its patients?* Available at: www.kingsfund.org.uk/sites/default/files/2018-06/NHS_at_70_what_will_new_technology_mean_for_the_NHS_0.pdf (downloaded 15.11.2018)

Charles, A. (2017). *Developing accountable care systems lessons from Canterbury, New Zealand*. Available at: www.kingsfund.org. uk/sites/default/files/2017-08/Developing_ACSs_final_digital_0. pdf (downloaded 15.11.2018)

Consilium Research & Consultancy. (2018). *Scoping study on the emerging use of Artificial Intelligence (AI) and Robotics in social care*. Available at: www.skillsforcare.org.uk/Documents/Topics/ Digital-working/Robotics-and-AI-in-social-care-Final-report.pdf (downloaded 15.11.2018)

Evans, J. M., Daub, S., Goldhar, J., Wojtak, A., & Purbhoo, D. (2016). Leading integrated health and social care systems: per-spectives from research and practice. *Healthcare Quality*, *18*(4), 30–35.

Fillingham, D., & Weir, B. (2014). *System leadership. Lessons and learning from AQuA's Integrated Care Discovery Communities*. Available at: www.kingsfund.org.uk/sites/default/files/field/field_ publication_file/system-leadership-october-2014.pdf (downloaded 11.11.2018)

Ghate, D., Lewis, J., & Welbourn, D. (2013). *Systems leadership: exceptional leadership for exceptional times*. Available at: www. cevi.org.uk/docs/Systems_Leadership_Synthesis_Paper.pdf (downloaded 11.11.2018)

Gullery, C., & Hamilton, G. (2015). Towards integrated person-centred healthcare: the Canterbury journey. *Future Hospital Journal*, *2*(2), 111–116.

House of Commons. (2018). *Accountable Care Organisations*. Available at: https://researchbriefings.parliament.uk/Research Briefing/Summary/CBP-8190 (downloaded 15.11.2018)

Local Government Association & IPC. (2016). *Transforming social care through the use of information and technology*. Available at: www.local.gov.uk/our-support/our-improvement-offer/care-and-health-improvement/informatics/transforming-care-through-tech nology (downloaded 15.11.2018)

Local Government Association, NHS Clinical Commissioners, NHS Providers & NHS Confederation. (2018). *Learning from the van-guards: spreading and scaling up change*. Available at: www.

nhsconfed.org/resources/2018/01/learning-from-vanguards-spreading-scaling-up-change (downloaded 11.11.2018)

McClellan, M., Kent, J., Beales, S. J., Cohen, S. I., Macdonnell, M., Thoumi, A., … Darzi, A. (2014). Accountable care around the world: a framework to guide reform strategies. *Health Affairs*, *33*(9), 1507–1515.

McClellan, M., Udayakumar, K., Thoumi, A., Gonzalez-Smith, J., Kadakia, K., Kurek, N., … Darzi, A. W. (2017). Improving care and lowering costs: evidence and lessons from a global analysis of accountable care reforms. *Health Affairs*, *36*(11), 1920–1927.

McMaster University. (2016). *Rapid synthesis: examining the impacts of Accountable Care Organizations on patient experience, population health and costs*. Available at: www.mcmasterforum.org/docs/default-source/product-documents/rapid-responses/examin ing-the-impacts-of-accountable-care-organizations-on-patient-experience-population-health-and-costs.pdf?sfvrsn=2 (downloaded 15.11.2018)

NHS Highland. (2018). *Update on eHealth to NHS Highland Board*. Available at: www.nhshighland.scot.nhs.uk/Meetings/BoardsMeet ings/Documents/July%202018/4.7%20eHealth%20Update.pdf (downloaded 15.11.2018)

Oshry, B. (1999). *Leading systems: lessons from the power lab*. Oakland: Berrett-Koehler Publishers.

Peiris, D., News, M., & Nallaiah, K. (2018). *Accountable Care Organisations*. Available at: www.aci.health.nsw.gov.au/__data/assets/pdf_file/0009/420939/ACO-Evidence-Check.pdf (downloaded 15.11.2018)

Pollock, A. M., & Roderick, P. (2018). Why we should be concerned about accountable care organisations in England's NHS. *BMJ*, *360*, k343.

Rogers, E. (16 August 2003). *Diffusion of innovations*. 5th Edition. New York: Simon and Schuster.

Scottish Government Health & Sport Committee. (2018). *Looking ahead to the Scottish Government – Health Budget 2019–20: is the budget delivering the desired outcomes for health and social*

care in Scotland? Available at: https://digitalpublications.parlia
ment.scot/Committees/Report/HS/2018/10/29/Looking-ahead-
to-the-Scottish-Government—Health-Budget-2019-20–Is-the-
budget-delivering-the-desired-outcomes-for-health-and-social-
care-in-Scotland- (downloaded 11.11.2018)

Senge, P., Hamilton, H., & Kania, J. (2015) The dawn of systems
leadership. *The Stanford Social Innovation Review*, Winter. Available at: https://ssir.org/articles/entry/the_dawn_of_system_lea
dership (downloaded 11.11.2018)

Vize, R. (2014). *The revolution will be improvised.* Available at:
www.leadershipcentre.org.uk/wp-content/uploads/2016/12/
Revolution-will-be-improvised-publication-v3.pdf   (downloaded
11.11.2018)

Welbourn, D., Warwick, R., Carnall, C., & Fathers, D. (2012). *Leadership of whole systems*. London: Kings Fund.

Welsh Government. (2018) *A Healthier Wales: our plan for health
and social care*. Available at: https://gov.wales/topics/health/pub
lications/healthier-wales/?lang=en (downloaded 11.11.2018)

World Health Organisation. (2015). *WHO global strategy on people-
centred and integrated health services*. Available at: www.who.int/
servicedeliverysafety/areas/people-centred-care/global-strategy/
en/ (downloaded 11.11.2018).

Index

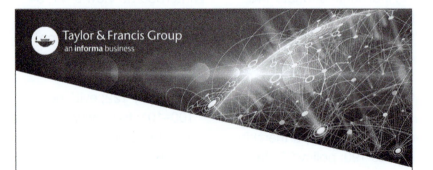